I0486300

2nd Edition

How to Shape Human Behavior

63 Specialists. 38 Agencies. 4 Countries. 662 Advertising,
Branding, Public Relations and User Experience Solutions

16 DEC 2014

Joshua Smith
www.humanbehavior.solutions

Thanks to Olivier Massanella for helping with the cover of this 2nd edition, and a very special thank you to the professionals who took the time to answer my questions for this 2nd Edition of How to Shape Human Behavior as well as those who didn't make this edition but will appear in future versions.

Joshua Smith

CONTENTS

PREFACE

How To Shape Human Behavior is a project nearly six years in the making, and has gone through several significant transformations during that time.

Originally, I set out to answer the question *'How can startups create their own advertising campaigns on a budget?'* I envisioned a manual that outlined step-by-step the creative process professional advertising agencies use to create advertising campaigns. All my early research centered around answering this question.

However the more I researched, the more I realized that I was asking the wrong question; I was merely scratching the surface of a deeper, more important question. And so I felt compelled to deepen the focus of my research.

Humans prefer consistency and predictability. It's evident in the products they repeatedly buy, the books they typically read, the beliefs they unquestionably defend. It shows in their logic and reasoning. In the short-term consistency and predictability make society run more smoothly. They make life easier and decisions safer. In fact, there are over a hundred other heuristics and cognitive biases that shape the way humans behave and make decisions. **How To Shape Human Behavior** addresses each and every one of those biases from an entrepreneur's perspective.

Why? Because successful entrepreneurs don't sell products and services; successful entrepreneurs shape human behavior. And for entrepreneurs, shaping human behavior begins from inside the consumer's mind. The more intimately you understand the mechanisms and complexities of human behavior, the more control you have over the future of your business decisions. In the hands of an entrepreneur, applicable knowledge of the human mind is priceless.

Whether you're a new startup creating your branding strategy or an established business looking to add a fresh new perspective to your brand, **How To Shape Human Behavior** takes you step-by-step through every phase of shaping human behavior needed to build a successful, consumer-centered business.

An important note. How To Shape Human Behavior is intentionally written as a guide to building a successful business through understanding and using human cognitive weakness that shape human behavior. There will no doubt be times when the offensive and defensive strategies and techniques outlined herein will make you feel uncomfortable or go against what you consider to be ethical behavior. Humans don't like the idea that they are being 'manipulated' into making decisions and giving their money to brands for any reason other than their own free will. But just because you may consider using this knowledge is unethical doesn't mean it doesn't work, and it doesn't mean that other entrepreneurs aren't currently using them to their advantage. It is critical for you to be able to distinguish between manipulation and persuasion. More importantly, it is crucial that your consumers correctly distinguish manipulation and persuasion when it comes to evaluating your brand and integrity.

The research in this book is based on academic research and interviews and discussions with professional marketers and executives. Careful attention has been made to accurately cite every reference used. All references are denoted in superscript so you can both verify the research as well as conduct your own.

Another important note. Before implementing any of the advice outlined herein, always consider how your message will be perceived by your target consumer demographic as well as the short- and long-term positive and negative implications your actions will have on your brand image. Most importantly, never do anything that would cause consumers to feel like you've tricked them.

Joshua M. Smith

HOW DOES THE ADVERTISING PROCESS WORK?

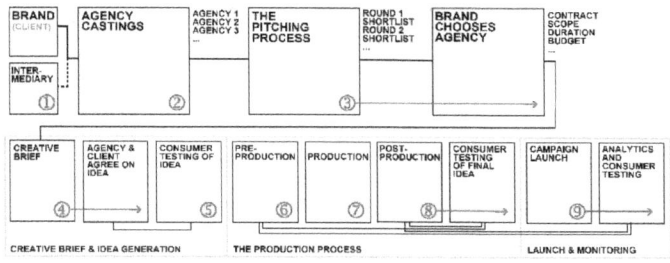

THE PITCHING PROCESS

① A brand contacts an intermediary agency who oversees the pitching process. The intermediary agency sits down with the brand and writes up a preliminary creative brief. This brief can be the actual brief the brand wants to solve, or a fake brief. The intermediary agency is also there to advise which agencies would be the best fit with the brand based on the brand's values, needs and to avoid conflict of interest. For example, advertising agencies cannot legally have two brands that are in direct competition with one another as clients (i.e. BMW and Mercedes). Brands may also choose to go directly to the different agencies.

② Next, the intermediary agency and the brand sit down with each agency individually for presentation and Q&A to see how the agency thinks. After meeting with each agency, the brand creates a shortlist of their favorite agencies.

1

③ Shortlisted agencies work from the creative brief created by the brand and the intermediary agency, and create one direction with two to three different executions for the brief to pitch to the client. With each round of pitching the shortlist gets smaller until the brand decides upon one agency. Once the contract has been negotiated, drawn up and signed, the intermediary agency is no longer involved in the process, and the brand now becomes the agency's client.

THE CREATIVE BRIEF & IDEA GENERATION

④ The client gives the agency a real marketing brief and the agency then turns that into a creative brief, strategic planners conduct market research and consumer testing to determine the best approach to answering the brief, and the creative team then comes up with two to three different possible solutions to solve the client's problem outlined in the brief. Mockups are made and presented to the client.

⑤ Step 4 may go through several rounds until the client decides upon one solution (direction with executions). Once the client has chosen, more consumer testing is conducted (by the agency, the client, or through an external company) until the client is comfortable that the idea will be well received by the public.

THE PRODUCTION PROCESS

⑥ Once the client gives the agency the go ahead, the agency then executes the idea – find models or actors, photographers or directors, location, lighting, make-up artists, clothing and set decoration, etc. Once all has been set up, the client confirms that all is okay during the pre-production meeting.

⑦ During production, the agency recreates the mockups agreed by the client as well as takes additional photos or footage so that there are more options available during post-production. Once production is over, the process moves into post-production.

⑧ In post-production, all of the material, photos, and videos made during production are pieced together and edited into a final version of the advertising campaign. More consumer testing may be conducted, and the client and the agency will be in back and forth meetings until the client is comfortable that the idea will be well received by the public. If consumer testing shows a negative response to the campaign, the client may return to the post-production to edit the final campaign or even start over in pre-production.

CAMPAIGN LAUNCH & MONITORING

⑨ As soon as the campaign has been launched, analytics are conducted to monitor the success of the campaign and further consumer testing may be conducted to see how the campaign can be further refined to adapt to the public and make the campaign more effective.

Depending on the campaign's analytics, consumer testing and the media's response to the advertisement, the client may return to the post-production stage to refine certain parts of the campaign, or may completely pull the campaign off air and return to the pre-production stage.

This process depends, of course, on the brand's goals, budget and time constraints.

I WANT TO HIRE A PROFESSIONAL. HOW CAN I TELL THE GOOD FROM THE BAD?

10. If you aren't very creative then you'll need to invest money in hiring somebody to create an idea for you. But if the person you hire gives you an idea that doesn't turn out to be remarkable, then you've lost your money on a mediocre idea and the money you do invest in placing your advertising will be wasted because consumers won't notice it.[58]

11. Most clients approach the advertising process by contacting a handful of agencies and launching a competition, inviting several agencies to pitch their idea. This process allows the brand and the advertising agency to decide whether or not they want to work with each other.

Clients familiar with this process tend to know exactly what information the agency needs to create a creative brief. Preparing this information in advance saves the client time and money. (Outlined later in this book).[49]

12. Clients often have difficulty putting into words what they really want – and then there is the matter of distinguishing what the client wants and what the client needs. When clients don't really know what they want, agencies often present case studies of what the client's competitors have been doing or what other interesting campaigns have been going on around the world to elicit ideas to help the client express what they want. This involves a bit of strategic planning.[60]

13. Obviously there isn't a simple magic formula to create your idea, image, product, and website, but there are some people who have learned how to consistently crack the code through experience and by using a number of different methods.[41]

14. Good creative directors have seen so many creative briefs, and have seen so many advertising situations that they instinctively 'know' when a creative brief is inspiring or not.[42]

15. Some clients can believe that advertising will solve all their problems as well as be:

    a. High-quality
    b. Quick
    c. Inexpensive

Advertising agencies do their best to provide all three, and there are those few magically creative ideas that accomplish all three, but more often than not brands must choose between two of them rather than having all three of these options. Meaning, if you want inexpensive, then your campaign can be quick but it probably won't be as high-quality as you'd like it to be. If you want it quick, then it will be expensive and maybe not as high of quality as you'd like it to be. If you want high-quality, then it probably can't be done inexpensively or quickly.[39]

16. A 360° campaign generally includes:

    a. Print
    b. Website
    c. Event (design, creation, and organization)
    d. Television
    e. Super-marketing (free samples or demonstrations)
    f. Phone apps
    g. Radio

360° campaigns are hard to sell nowadays because clients want to work with specialists. The problem is that an agency will do an excellent print campaign for one client, an excellent TV campaign for another client, and an excellent viral campaign for a third client; and each client won't realize that the agency can also do the other types of campaigns. It's not until the agency actually provides case studies, statistics and proof of what the agency has done for other clients that the client understands the agency's full capabilities and accepts to work together on other, larger projects.

If you're looking for a 360° campaign, then you have to think in terms of the campaign as a whole, not just the individual components of it. Working with one agency on every platform ensures a more coherent campaign because everything is done and thought of under the same roof and by the same group of people. Also the final campaign will cost significantly less because agencies offer lower prices for package deals, whereas trying to patchwork a 360° campaign with several agencies will cost more in the long run.[49]

17. Big ad agencies are usually full-service: they have everything needed to create and implement creative advertising campaigns in-house. This saves time and money, but can lead to a sort of group think since everyone in the organization is used to working and creating together.

Medium to smaller agencies and freelancers can't afford to do everything in-house, so must outsource some of the creative process. This can make it more expensive but this can also provide many different angles from different people who'll contribute to your project. [47]

18. Agencies never tell a client something is impossible, because nothing is impossible anymore! There are degrees of difficulty given a budget, timeframe, and other applications that need to be integrated, etc., but nothing is impossible. This is a very recent phenomenon; three or four years ago, 'impossible' was still in the agency's vocabulary. [41]

19. In the long run, working in advertising does eventually become mundane and you lose inspiration. So be aware that this is natural, and know when you need to take a break from the industry or move on to other things. Don't wait until you become so burned out and are no longer capable of producing quality advertising ideas that your agency has to let you go.

Creatives who have lost their creative edge and have nothing to fall back on may go freelance. So clients must learn to identify when a creative has burned out. [48]

20. A lot of projects (advertising, web design, etc.) look artificial, and there are a lot of 'brand identity gurus' out there that give you the feeling that they're offering products that they don't seem to really believe in, and so they embellish and overstate things. [50]

21. Advertising can become overwhelming, and it's frustrating the amount of unprofessional and low quality banner ads out there, being as anybody can create an ad and pay to have it circulate in Google AdSense. [38]

22. Ad agencies aren't all the same. Depending on the company and network you're in, you can have different perceptions of what quality advertising is and isn't. Ad agencies can have different cultures and selling propositions. [15]

23. It might not be necessary to be a good web developer to run a website, but it is one important element of many. There are plenty of people who are not very good web developers and not even necessarily good web designers, but they're good at using the tools available to them, and if their design and message are good enough their idea or brand will get picked up and spread everywhere.[41]

24. There's a world of spectacularly talented people out there who do things differently than you or I and we get to work with them; this is simultaneously humbling and exciting.[26]

25. Ask around and take advantage of word of mouth. As creatives get older and develop a reputation for the quality of their work, they will be less and less asked for their portfolio. Or you can simply Google them and find work they've done. But when creatives are younger, their portfolio is their calling card.[48]

26. Don't necessarily rely on prizes and awards the creative may have been a part of. This is because independent freelancers cannot enter their work into award competitions – only agencies can. This means that if the freelancer has been freelance for several years, any awards he or she may have won several years prior only reflect the quality of that freelancer's previous work while he or she was working with a team of other qualified professionals while employed at an award-winning advertising agency. The freelancer in question may very well have been the weakest link in the agency, which is why he or she no longer works at the agency... It's something to think about.[53]

27. Always look at the agency's homepage. They need to have a homepage. They can't just have an 'about me' page or a cargo collective page. They need to

have something that they have hopefully coded themselves, or have at least personalized if they haven't coded it themselves and maybe gotten someone else to do it for them. That's number one.[50]

28. Don't just look at whether their work is 'good,' look at the idea behind the ads in the agency's portfolio. If the ideas aren't good for the selection of projects he or she specifically chose to show you, then you can assume that the idea he or she will choose for your project will be just as bad. Learning to tell the difference between good and bad advertising ideas takes practice. Once you can spot the difference, you can adequately qualify the agency's portfolio.[53]

29. Consider how the agency shows off its work. The person may know a lot of relevant or impressive websites or may be able to drop a lot of names but not actually show anything off. If it isn't already on their website, ask for a list of companies they have worked for as well as companies they want to work for. People do get busy, but the number one red flag when if you're looking to hire someone for web or mobile is that that person doesn't have their own personal online portfolio. That is step number one in showing that you actually care about the internet.[50]

30. There are unscrupulous advertisers, creative directors and copywriters who intentionally steal other people's work and try to pass it off as their own, hoping nobody will notice; however most idea theft usually isn't done on purpose. It's just that nearly all advertisers are working from the same intellectual thought processes stemming from the same books of techniques, graduating from the same advertising school curriculums, and using the same consumer-base demographic to create their advertising campaigns.[48]

Take your time and choose who you work with wisely. But once you have made your decision, trust their judgment.

31. There are two billing models agencies use when it comes to pitching to clients: Some agencies pitch for free, while others refuse to pitch for free, and bill the client for the amount of hours spent on the project 'thus far.'[49]

32. Good ideas work regardless of the size of your budget, and many professional agencies work for free for non-profit organizations in exchange for creative freedom. This is because most paying clients impose demands and limitations as to what their advertising can be. This can be frustrating for creatives who dislike limitations on creativity. So if you're willing to give advertising agencies the freedom to do an edgy project not confined by rules and requirements, they might work for almost free. If you don't have money, give them the freedom to create something interesting. Money isn't [#]1 for creatives.[1]

33. Consider it a red flag for you if an agency's answer to your creative brief is *"Unless you have a budget of $5M, I'm absolutely useless to you."* [44]

34. When pitching ideas to a client, agencies usually present at least three ideas. Any less and the presentation seems poor; the client feels like the agency didn't put enough time and thought into the client's needs and that the client isn't getting their money's worth. On the contrary if agencies provide too many options or ideas, the agency risks appearing as though they aren't confident with their design and the direction they want to go, which is also a waste of money on both the client's and the agency's part.[60]

35. One of the revisions clients nearly always request when they see the first draft of an ad is to *'make the logo bigger.'* However simply making the logo bigger risks taking away from the power of the brand message. Knowing this, art directors can intentionally make the logo smaller in the first draft than it should be, that way when the client demands a bigger logo, the art director can adjust the logo to its ideal size and everyone is happy.[45]

36. Most of the time planners aren't involved in tactical or business-centric campaigns such as "30% off promotions" or slight adaptations of already existing advertising campaigns that don't require a strategic brief. However whenever there is significant money and branding reputation involved, this is when strategic planners step in.[42]

37. The agency's creative team (strategic planners, art directors and copywriters), the ones who actually create your campaign, may have worked for multiple different agencies throughout their career, so the most important test is to ask questions about the agency's philosophy to see if it is in line with yours. If your ideals and vision align, then the ad agency is probably a good match.[47]

38. It does happen that creatives must create advertising campaigns for products of which they aren't the target consumer. Therefore what the art director likes may not be of much importance to the campaign.[45]

39. Every single decision you make affects how a user will view and use your product/website.[50]

40. A lot of this requires knowledge into how consumers and brands think and reason, and then working around that.[45]

41. The whole job of marketing is to turn human understanding into business advantage - hence it is the agency's job above all else to be at the forefront of any new insights into how people decide and act.[44]

42. The agency should be more interested in the client's consumer than the client because the agency's job is to increase the client's sales. Often times the agency will hear the client say *"I was looking for another campaign idea, but yours increased sales, so I'm happy."*[17]

43. Trust is key. You should know and trust that the advertising agency is serious and truly understands your business. You should feel like the ad agency is a partner working at the same company, not like some external consulting company.[13]

44. Be careful about whose advice you take. But if you haven't thought about your strategy (where am I going?) or about identity (who am I?) then, as far as the agency is concerned, you don't have a full proposition.[55]

45. Sitting through meetings, reassuring the client, giving presentations and winning pitches...the agency's relationship with client is extremely important to the success of the campaign.[45]

46. Quality advertising agencies see their contract with a client as a relationship. Meaning, if you come to the agency with a small budget but with an idea the agency believes in, the agency may be willing to work within your constraints as best they can because they believe in your brand, and because the value of their relationship with you will come to fruit in other ways, such as creating an award winning campaign or the chance to be on the ground floor of the next big viral brand.[46]

47. The breakthrough in a true client-agency relationship is the willingness to pause in the process when we believe we are not doing our best work and talk about it.[26]

48. Ultimately, the agency is paid to sell the client's product, not to sell itself. So in the end the agency gives the client what the client wants.[45]

49. Overall, advertising isn't based on tangible things, it's based on ideas.[15]

50. Agencies bill clients not only depending on the amount of time spent on the client's project, but also on the profitability of the idea. The problem is it's often quite difficult to place the right value on an idea. Sometimes great ideas can take shape in very little time but it can permit the client to earn ALOT of money. Other times ideas take a lot of time and in the end not earn as much as expected. The problem is accurately determining the value of an idea and the steps involved in realizing the idea.[4]

51. The agency creating the concept (logo and tagline together) generally maintains the creative rights to the produced work, and the client cannot just simply do what they want with the concept of the creation. Ownership of concept should be clearly outlined in your contract.

When a logo is created, guidelines for the logo usage are usually also created by the agency that created the logo. These guidelines can be as many as 40-50 pages outlining everything from:

a. The minimum and maximum allowable size of the logo
b. Logo placement on a product
c. Logo placement on posters

d. Color palates of secondary colors that can be used with the logo
e. The minimum size of secure area (blank space) around the logo
f. The typeface limitations and requirements for print and office typeface advertising medium
g. The chromatic palette compatibility with the color of the logo on stationary, badges, faxes, memos, brochures, correspondence cards, envelopes, etc. and business cards as well as the company's address, telephone number, service department, etc.

These guidelines are created to control your brand image and strategy.[12]

52. The creative industry is changing. Brands will always need creative people to come up with the innovative ideas behind product designs, advertising and branding campaigns, but it's possible that in the future there will be fewer and fewer 'professional creatives' and technology will automate more and more aspects of the creative process from the creative brief to the final product.[48]

WHAT MISCONCEPTIONS DO BRANDS COMMONLY HAVE ABOUT MARKETING?

BRANDING STRATEGY

53. Brand yourself as select and confidential, at least at the beginning. Later, once you've branded yourself, you can open your brand up if you want to the general public without losing that sentimental feeling of exclusivity and special treatment. [35]

54. Brands usually have two or three peak sales times during the year depending on the type of product they're commercializing (back to school and Christmas for kids, Valentine's Day, etc.). Activation is about obtaining higher visibility during those peak sales times. Because brands don't aggressively push sales year-round, brand activation is simply 'activating' your brand during those peak moment(s) to maximize exposure while your product is in highest demand.[61]

55. Typical components of brand activation can include, but are not limited to:

   a. Creating a website landing page that acts as the headquarters for your brand activation campaign.
   b. Launching a contest or giveaway (online or offline) as an incentive for consumers (current and potential) to engage with your brand.
   c. Organizing an event around your brand and product.

    d. Creating content – articles, videos, etc. – to inform, help and/or entertain consumers.

    e. Handing out coupons in and around the sales point.

But brand activation is much, much bigger than simply launching a giveaway and then driving people to your landing page to sign up. Brand activation is about meeting an objective; it's about actively taking control of your consumer's image of your brand by creating an experience around it as a way of explaining your brand's core values, vision and unique selling point as well as showcasing your products.[61]

56. If your objective is generating conversions such as collecting email addresses, then you might consider activating your brand every three months or so. But if you're selling a product, then product demand (i.e. the high sales points during the year) will dictate when you should invest most heavily in activation.[61]

57. If you sell more than one product, and if those products' peak sales fall at different times during the year, then you'll need to have separate activations for each product.[61]

58. Platform is key. You have to have a platform, and the platform has to be sustainable and feed itself. You have to have something from which to stand on. Focus on one thing at a time, then once that platform becomes self-sustaining revenue you can grow, branch out and branch off.[20]

59. The more your brand becomes iconic, the harder you have to work to avoid becoming a commodity.[39]

60. Stay up-to-date with everything relevant to your brand as best as you can, and then learn from your mistakes, adapt, and move on. You'll find that your followers and consumers will be more lenient with you than you realize. You might even find that what you thought was a mistake, and what statistics told you was a mistake, turns out to be a huge success; there are no rules![39]

61. Developing a good reputation in your industry goes a long way for your career.[42]

62. The industry isn't static and you must always adapt to changing technology and the way you do business with clients.[13]

63. If you are competing in an industry where consumers are known to have a high level of brand loyalty, you cannot compete by advertising or creating a truly unique packaging design. Instead, you must be innovative.[46]

64. Branding is about positioning your brand, and then advertising acts as a way of nudging and influencing consumers.[51]

65. To put things in order of importance for businesses launching a new product:

   a. Branding strategy
   b. Creative brief for problem to solve
   c. Product or service
   d. Pricing
   e. Product design congruent to pricing
   f. Advertising[51]

66. For consumers to know you exist you might do a public relations campaign. But really you need to invest in the quality of your idea. Consumers will remember ideas and how you make them feel. So you really want a strong branding idea that can translate from public relations to advertising. An advertisement built on an emotional idea will be remembered more than an advertisement without an emotional idea (for example a sales promotion). The idea is what makes you laugh, smile and feel emotion. Consumers will remember that. The only point of publicity is to make consumers remember.[51]

67. Choose a name that means nothing because if later you decide to branch out and do something different, you can. If your name is too narrow then you're limiting what you can do.[51]

68. There are many ways to create a branding strategy depending on the context: Are you a new brand? Are you an established brand wanting a re-brand?[42]

69. Disruption is perhaps a different word for what behavioral economic enthusiasts would call a "radical reframing strategy." I'm not fond of the term "emotional branding" because, quite frankly, what other kind of branding is there?[44]

70. Have an idea about how you want to position your brand or product: i.e. funny, serious, etc. This is outlined in your creative brief.[53]

71. Even if your brand's products and services are relatively the same as your competitors, each brand has its own unique history and story that makes it unique from every other product or service in its industry.[53]

72. Create your very own unique selling proposition (USP) by focusing your advertising around your brands:

    a. Product/Brand name
    b. Physical characteristics
    c. Logo/Identity
    d. Packaging
    e. Taste/Flavor
    f. Heritage/History/Reputation
    g. Price
    h. How your product is eaten or used
    i. Competition
    j. How your product is made
    k. Key ingredients
    l. Product lifespan
    m. Personality
    n. Attitude
    o. Already existing advertising
    p. Your consumer
    q. You, the owner or your staff[53]

73. You have so much more to offer than the mere products and services you sell. Explore every niche and aspect at your disposition and research every angle you have to build a business.[56]

74. Know your market and your competitors. How can you really distinguish yourself as a superior product if you have no idea what your competitors are offering?[56]

75. Consistency is also very important in regards to how people recognize you as a brand. They see your unique and familiar website design or product

design with your familiar logo on it and consumers know immediately where they are. Also the use of your logo must be consistent. The factor of recognition is important in a world of visual information overflow.[54]

76. If you only draw inspiration and references from a small niche of life, you may be able to attract that particular niche of people, but you'll be missing out, and even alienating, everyone else. Create advertising that everyone can see themselves in and relate to; even if your product is for a niche market. This is how advertising campaigns go viral. [53]

77. Trust that you know your target audience and that you know what is best for your business.[56]

78. Compare what you offer with your competitors and look at their pricing structure. For any business you really have to charge a certain amount if you want to attract a certain type of customer.[56]

79. You need a strong logo before you need a strong packaging design and advertising presence.[58]

BUSINESS MODELS

80. When you start your own online business, your customers become your boss. But as a website owner, you're no longer tied to the fluxuating local economy.[16]

81. Sometimes people think that everything is possible without understanding the process enough to know that it takes time and money to do a proper job.[33]

82. Don't expect instant results. Just keep putting yourself out there. Make contacts and build a network. Use whatever you have at your disposal. Eventually you'll reach a point where you can spend less time marketing and more time creating quality projects. But this is thanks to years of putting networking first and building a contact directory.[36]

83. Even if you're not good at what you do, you only have your own sensibility and taste. Don't think that your point of view is the only point of view. Your idea is your baby, not everyone else's baby. Listen to other people and be humble - understand their point of view.[1]

84. Never assume things. Confirm everything! If you're unsure about anything, always ask! Even if you're sure, confirm.[6]

85. Don't work for nothing. You have to know how to determine what's urgent and what can wait. Things inevitably change, even after the contract is signed. Take your time because things will change frequently. Sit back and once you feel you're finished changing your mind, then it's time to go to work.[12]

86. If your time management and data flow is bad, you can easily get overloaded and then not stay up-to-date.[13]

87. Watching your costs is more important than anything else.[16]

88. What worked before probably won't work again, at least to the same effect.[16]

89. Beware of the shiny objects syndrome. Entrepreneurs tend to have a lot of excellent ideas. Store them away and come back to them later when you've finished what you're currently doing.[20]

90. Nobody is irreplaceable. Never think to yourself *"I made it!"* because you can be on the top of the world today and lose everything tomorrow morning. Always question yourself.[24]

91. When you do a direct marketing campaign by email you know who opened your email, who clicked on your link, how long each person stayed on your site, and how long they watched your video or read your content.[28]

92. Like in any job, problems become solutions, and today's problems become your key to expediency and ease tomorrow.[41]

93. Start from the transaction out. Don't start with advertising. Start close-in to the point of sale and work outwards. What are the barriers that prevent customers from doing business with you?[44]

94. Running a crowdfunding campaign isn't just sitting back and watching money come in - it's a full time job in itself. You have so much to handle because you have to simultaneously manage all aspects of the project - design, brand, promotion, social networking, press, etc.[43]

95. Spend more time, effort, and money searching for 'trim tab interventions' - very small things that have much bigger disproportionate effects.[44]

96. One of the great pieces of progress in meteorology is that they haven't just gotten better at forecasting, they've also gotten better at knowing what they simply **cannot** predict.[44]

97. Never do anything that could cause your user to feel like you've tricked them.[50]

98. Be as transparent and honest as you can be. If you can't do it, tell them. If you don't think their idea is a good idea, tell them and then tell them why you think that. Even if they decide not to take your advice, they'll see that you have their best interest in mind. That really goes a long way.[52]

99. The efficiency of your emailings, banner ads and pre-roll videos really depends on your brand and target demographic. It depends on your brand, your target audience, the content of your banner ad, and the objective of your banner ad. Banner ads are but one of many tools, and they do work in certain circumstances.[52]

100. Constantly set yourself new challenges.[54]

101. Consider not creating an 'about me' section because pre-made answers and explanations could diminish the chance for consumers to have an experience that is as genuine as possible. Always be curious of how people perceive what they see on your website. If someone is interested in getting more information about you after they have visited your website, they can always contact you.[54]

102. People will always find a reason to complain; so go with your heart.[56]

103. You're not bound to only French clients just because you live in France.[56]

104. 80% of what you do doesn't bring in any immediate revenue. But if it weren't for all of that unpaid work you wouldn't be able to launch your next products. Everything you do should build upon what you've created before.[57]

105. Just launch! If you want to start a community, do it! What's the worst that can happen? Worst case scenario it fails, and if it fails it'll be forgotten about this time next year.[57]

106. Be passionate about what you're doing and truly believe in what you offer because passion is contagious and inspiring. Even if your competitors do what you do better than you and have more experience, the right people will see your passion and will invest in you and get behind you.[57]

107. Separate professional and private life. Running a community can easily consume your entire life! Set times dedicated to your private life and do not work. Do not sacrifice relationships with the ones you love for the sake of business. Keeping your partner involved in your projects and goals certainly helps create a supportive home environment.[57]

108. Make yourself redundant. Identify the leaders who naturally emerge within your community and offer

them to become admin, official event organizers, or content writers. This allows you to focus on growing and improving the community, services and projects and your members have more things to do.

Sub-communities will even begin to emerge inside of your community.[57]

109. Keep improving. Building your business is a learn-as-you-go process. Be patient, learn from your mistakes and from the mistakes of others and constantly change and improve upon your idea until you find the right approach. Don't wait for everything to be perfect, it will never be the perfect time to launch any project/community/service, there will always be something that can be better but you have plenty of time to rectify it.[57]

110. Keep building. While your clients and community members are aware of your existing plans, try to envision what's missing in the market and plan for it. Keep one eye on how all of your activities will allow you to launch future projects. Your largest and riskiest project should always take place the next 18-24 months...[57]

111. Every self-made wealthy person always have the same answer:

   a. Find people who will pay you more than you pay them, and/or
   b. Find people who will pay you continuously. In terms of posting articles and videos online: Do something one time, get paid forever.[16]

112. Websites and blogging aren't a get rich quick scheme, but they pay off in the long run. Stay

committed and just write really good articles. The readers will come. Make sure you're sharing, being social, and responding to comments. The readership will come.[20]

113. Fame doesn't always equal money. A lot of times you have to choose between one and the other. Many well-known bloggers and tweeters aren't the wealthiest people, whereas many lesser-known, marginal internet marketers whom nobody knows are loaded with cash. At some point you may have to choose what it is you're actually looking for: fame or fortune. It can be very difficult to have both.[20]

114. Be patient. The only reason you do things in your passion is because you're going to be more patient when things don't happen the way you want them to.

If you do something that's out of your passion because it's a better market, you'll give up faster.[20]

115. Do you just want to make money or actually help people?[16]

116. A lot of people, 'gurus' especially, find ideas and keep it to themselves or charge a lot of money for them. Don't blindly believe what all the gurus are saying. You have no idea how quickly marketing strategies change. Online marketing changes on a month-to-month basis and search engine results can fluxuate significantly depending on Google's messing around with their algorithm and other things.[16]

117. Prioritize your responsibilities and dedicate yourself to the project at hand without getting distracted. To be efficient you have to be dedicated to what you're doing at the moment, and avoid skipping from one subject to another as much as possible - make every minute count.[5]

118. Develop your operational and tactical international strategy:

    a. **Tactical** means how your brand reaches your target market and objectives- sales, position, revamping, etc. It's about finding a problem to solve, researching the problem, and then solving it.

    b. **Operational** means managing all of your day-to-day responsibilities of your campaign from preparing your creative brief to coordinating with the creatives and planners: all of the links in the advertising chain.[6]

119. Think of any major industry and you can probably name one or two CEOs. Whenever there's an international matter, journalists are always interested in having a thought leader's opinion and impression. Maybe a particular company isn't #1 in its industry, but you know the company because you've seen their CEO and you've heard him/her being interviewed. The CEO may have only been a reference, but when CEOs manage to reach that level it brings added value to their company.[28]

120. You're in business to make money for whatever reason, we all know this. The question is how are you making money, what is your purpose. This is very interesting to think about. It makes you fundamentally look at what you're doing and examine how you can do it better. Ask yourself *"What is my purpose?"*[2]

121. Find your own business model to win and keep your clients, and keep adapting and adapting so you don't get overtaken by a new market contender.[35]

122. Don't spend a single dime until you've exhausted your branding strategy and industry analysis identifying the right target demographic, the right media, and the cleverest way to reach your target demographic.[34]

123. The better your CEO-value, the better your company image. All other things constant, the better communicator conveys confidence and trust, and so usually has a better image in his/her industry. That is a valuable asset to any company. When comparing two companies in the same sector, the company with a poor CEO value usually has a poorer stock performance than the company with a higher CEO value.[28]

124. The better organized and prepared your brand is, the less time and money you waste, and the more powerful your campaigns will be because advertising agencies can focus all of their creative craft solving your precise problem.[49]

125. We live in an era where people are used to not paying for anything on the web: music, movies, news, information… it's all free. Further, many people are willing to settle for low quality content that is free than high-quality content that they have to pay for. You cannot stop it, so rather than fight it you should absorb it into your business model.

Place our logo on all your content and consider people's using our content on their website as free advertising for your brand. It's easier to absorb it than to fight it.[30]

126. In-house can be quite a conundrum. On the one hand you have the luxury of being completely immersed in your brand's needs and goals, which can lead to the freedom to tell your brand's story in the most creative and cost effective way possible - ingenuity at its best. BUT, on the other hand you're steeped so deep your brand's goals and needs that you can't always see solutions because you're looking out from the inside. On the agency side clients come to external advertising agencies because of those blind spots.[26]

127. Be professional. Do the best work you can and to be proud of what you create, but remember your place in the grand scheme of things.[27]

128. Bad (branding, economic, business, etc.) models, once they've become widely accepted, have an extraordinary capacity to survive - through a kind of lazy consensus.[44]

129. Economics has this weird thing in that so many people have careers, advancement, and promotion dependent on basically believing in neoclassical economics and its propagation that it's become a sort of pseudo-scientific religion. Once you've invested a lot of effort in learning the lingo, you're pretty reluctant to abandon it.[44]

130. Document everything. Always maintain a written record of events, conversations, meeting objectives, agreements and obligations, etc. This ensures there isn't any confusion.[34]

131. You cannot expect to have your family and social life separated from your work life. It's all related.[30]

132. Be more picky with who you do business with. Choose people not because they can help you, but because they're qualified in what they do.[30]

133. Expect to periodically make dumb mistakes up until the very end. It just happens. To minimize that, really be careful before committing to anything. If there's any way to test the waters before you spend a huge chunk of money, do it.[29]

134. There are TONS of startups that fail to tell you what they do. When that happens, it's generally because the company itself doesn't know how to articulate their product vision.[50, 51]

135. Brands want to be known as the best in everything. But this is simply not possible. Brands cannot be everything to everyone, nor can they be everywhere all the time; so this is among the first questions I ask the brand *'What exactly are you, and who are you?'*[49]

136. Some brands don't like taking risks with their image and prefer the 'tried and true' methods to advertising.[42]

137. Many of the first creative briefs agencies receive from clients want *"an idea that is absolutely revolutionary – the next big idea that really pushes the envelope and pushes the brand to the next level!"*

Fair enough. But as the campaign moves through the various stages (pre-production, production, post-production...), the closer and closer to a finished product the agency gets, coupled with consumer testing, that 'risky' attitude outlined in the original brief slowly dissipates as the thought of *"what if this risky idea actually ruins our brand!?"* starts to sink in.[60]

Therefore most of the time clients want advertising that is calm and risk-free. Everyone is trying to keep their job, so nobody is willing to take risks. So agencies must do their best to convince brands that risk is necessary to make something unique and differentiate themselves from their competition.[47]

138. Clients tend to make their advertising less and less interesting because it's less risky, and in this economy they want to be safe. Brands don't want to offend anyone and they want to save money. They want to sell more products without taking risks.[49]

139. Globally, the way companies set up rewards systems means that they are sort of doomed to lose their talented people after a certain number of years. They won't keep innovating forever, people will move to other companies, and their product will slowly lose value.[50]

140. You should always strive to take your idea one step further. The day you can no longer find any fault in what you've created, you should be worried.[58]

141. Brands lacking a clear vision, brand identity, corporate structure, and/or are unorganized internally as to exactly who makes the final decision waste a lot of time and money simply because of the number of revisions it takes for the advertising agency to create a campaign that satisfies the brand.

That being said, a brand that doesn't have a clear vision, in the hands of competent and professional advertisers, might actually turn out to be an advantage because the brand will be more open to creative ideas and solutions. This may actually result in a better, more original advertising campaign, whereas brands who *'know exactly what they want'* and refuse to consider other options outside of what they want may pay less, but they may also be missing out on some incredible solutions which could have a greater reach and return on investment.[49]

142. *"I want a campaign that uses the color green."* Well, why do you want green? Because green shows nature, organic, etc.? Then *"I want to show how my product is natural and organic"* is a better brief that agencies can work with because there are thousands of better ways to show natural and organic than by simply using the color green.[60]

143. You already have something that people want. It might be something you own, something you've learned how to do, or access to valuable resources, space, or people.[59]

144. You should have a sketch notebook and a pencil with you at all times.[58]

145. When you're a company just starting out, don't worry too much about the logo – don't spend any significant amount of time or money on it because you can always change it later. Brands are constantly updating their logos and they're doing fine.[50]

146. Brands should refresh their image around every 5 years. That being said, if you have a timeless logo and typography, NEVER change it! If it works, don't change it.[58]

147. Brands that understand awareness and the need to create awareness tend to be more open to non-Cartesian ideas.[52]

148. Most very early startups with little to no marketing budget rely on their friends supporting them or through public relations.[50]

149. Some brands, and some representatives of the brand, either have no idea how the branding process works or have preconceived notions as to how the process is supposed to work.[49]

150. Clients don't always realize that there is an entire process involved behind-the-scenes before agencies present our final idea(s) to them. Some clients can have a difficult time paying for brainstorming and creation time they can neither touch nor feel, but in the end once the agency presents them with a final tangible product that is specifically catered to theirs and their target consumer's demands, that's when brands are ready and willing to invest their money.[60]

151. Thinking that one little modification to an artwork would take only a minute is a major misconception.

The general argument is *"I could have done this on PowerPoint in less than a minute."* Often, the client doesn't realize that sometimes changing a little thing involves changing the whole artwork. The only way brands can avoid these problems in post-production is to anticipate every possible situation and have the photographer take the additional photos just in case or, more effectively, present temporary artwork to the client during pre-production and only proceed to the shooting or illustration phase once everything has been approved.[60]

152. Don't expect your launch to be an event. Nobody cares about your launch. In fact, don't even launch, just begin.[59]

153. Nothing is ever truly finished; everything can be improved upon. Finding improvements means finding weak points that can be corrected. But that doesn't give you permission to hold off launching your creation until it is 'perfect.' You must and should have time and budget constraints.[58]

154. Clients often say in their creative brief *'I want a viral advertising to increase my sales.'* Viral advertising can make your brand famous, but that doesn't mean it will increase sales.[52]

155. Advertising isn't a perfect science so you must believe something is going to work, and be aware that it might not work. You have to take the risk. With brands that do not want to take the risk; it shows in their advertising.[52]

156. Sometimes clients don't listen to their agency's advice and recommendations. Brands that approach a digital agency with the idea of *"This is what I want, now go and do it"* are missing out on a lot of opportunities.[52]

157. It's very hard to have an idea that speaks to everyone because ideas are funny or intelligent **because** they contain something that the target audience must already know before seeing the advertisement. You must speak to the specific audience who "understands and gets" the idea.

If you want to speak to everyone, your idea needs to be understood by everyone. That being said, brands that want to speak to everyone tend to be the most difficult to work with and, consequently, the more generic their advertising tends to be. The more specific your target, the more commonalities they share, and the more ideas you can build with.[51]

PRODUCTS, SERVICES & PACKAGING DESIGN

158. There can be a tendency for a brand to think that other people are <u>as</u> interested in their product as the brand is, which isn't always the case. A person's new product is their baby, but not necessarily so for other people. Other people don't live for your products, and sometimes brands don't have the sense of reality for what other people really want - what's important for other people.

Therefore sometimes you have to calm down and understand that it takes time for other people to get as excited about your product as you are.[1]

159. Don't undercharge. Have an idea of what you're worth and don't be afraid to charge it. You'll be tempted to undercharge because you want to get the job, but that gives you a lower opinion of yourself.[36]

160. In many industries and cultures, offering consulting services may be best received when you wrap a product around it. Make a product out of your service so your clients can touch it and see it. This makes it easier for consumers to pay a premium for your service when it comes along with, or at least resembles, a product.[28]

161. Some products and ideas are instant hits, and some are destined to be bad forever. Your goal is to learn to understand creation. The more you see GOOD creation, the better you become at spotting good creation from the bad. Surround yourself with only the best creations and products and websites and creative people so you have something to strive for, and this also helps you develop your instinct. Follow creative people so you constantly have good creative ideas streaming in front of your eyes. Sooner or later it will rub off on you. And don't only follow advertising, follow everything.[33]

162. Your product and packaging design are your brand's story in the flesh.[58]

163. You cannot create your packaging design until you've created your typography, color schema and logo.[58]

164. Logos don't really matter as much as agencies say they do. Some of the most powerful companies in the world have some of the tiniest, crappiest logos. It comes down to sheer repetition. You can have the most wonderful and beautifully designed logo in the world, and you're company will never be known – it's not some magical turnkey that some companies sell it as.

That being said, don't have a cheesy logo unless you have a children's company. Don't try to make it warm and fuzzy and encapsulate six different ideas – it's just one market.[50]

165. Be creative in how you differentiate yourself from your competitors.[46]

166. Your packaging design has to fit your price. If there is any incongruence between the price of your product and your product's perceived value, the consumer will notice the inconsistency and probably won't take the risk.[46]

167. It's important to understand the history of typography. Not every graphic designer knows this, but it's very important because typography evolves alongside technology, and the shape of typography is created by technology. We now have millions of different types, but not all of them are good.[46]

168. Typography is like a picture. It's necessary to buy it if you plan to use it commercially. A lot of people think typography is free, but somebody created that typography, and if you use somebody else's creation without the owner's expressed permission, you're at risk for copyright infringement, just like if you use someone else's picture or music without permission. Good typography is worth its price.[46]

169. There are two types of product packaging:

    a. To protect your product during shipping and handling and is then thrown into the trash. This is 90% of the packaging out there today.

    b. For decoration that you want to keep – a bottle of tea that you'll reuse to put more tea into afterwards because it looks beautiful in your kitchen and you needed somewhere to put your tea anyway.[46]

170. There are many books available that offer hundreds of cut-out package foldable models of packages that already exist. Find a handful of packaging models that you like and use them to create your own unique packaging design, and then figure out how to color and design it. Found a packaging you like? Very carefully disassemble it to see what it looks like when you unfold it.[46]

171. Your images have to be spectacular, whatever they are. Narratives and affiliations have to be crafted with care and intent. If your brand isn't willing to sell a shoddy product then why would you settle for a shoddy online destination?[26]

172. Don't invest money into a PR or advertising campaign until your visitors' experience on your website is attractive, relevant, and designed to convert.[29]

173. Your blog should request something from your visitor, the "call to action." This leads to your conversion rate. Your objective could be for the visitor to:

a. Subscribe to your RSS
b. Make a donation
c. Share your page
d. Give you their email address
e. Download something
f. Other [32]

174. For a visual identity, start with your logo. Spend a lot of time on the design of your typography and sign if there is one. It must be intelligent and encapsulate your brand personality. Everything must be simple; the simpler the better. For example, your logo and sign are the first thing people notice on a business card.[58]

175. New and refreshed logos and product designs should be accompanied by advertising and PR campaigns to get the word out.[58]

176. Put your colors and graphic shapes which accentuate your brand personality. It's very important to choose a good font (or fonts) from a reputable foundry. Typography is a very important graphic element that should not be taken lightly. A serif, sans-serif, or condensed version of the same typography can alter the entire identity of your brand.[58]

177. After you've chosen your typography choose your color scheme. Your competitors will have already claimed a certain color scheme, so you want to choose colors that accentuate your brand identity without coming across as a copycat.[58]

178. After you've chosen your color scheme choose the shape of your packaging design.[58]

179. You must distinguish between designing packaging for a one-time limited-edition package and designing for a product line. The point of a limited-edition is that it stands out from your brand's normal identity. But when you're designing a product line you have to factor in congruency among the different packaging design. Your packaging must be different enough that consumers can distinguish among your different products yet close enough that they can clearly recognize your brand.[58]

180. If you're a startup launching your first product, you can't expect to turn a one-time or limited-edition packaging design into a product line identity; you must plan far enough down the line to know whether you will offer extensions.[58]

181. Consider the packaging material you'll be using. Plastic? Paper? Metal? Will it be coated with a shiny or glittery substance?[58]

182. Keep your overall form, typography, layout and primary color of the packaging the same and then change your secondary color.[58]

183. Don't believe that packaging design is easy and quicker to design with today's technology. Yes, in two minutes you could change the color, but colors have meanings and competitors use certain colors and color combinations for very important branding reasons.[46]

184. Some brands believe that a design agency's advice on how the brand should change their packaging is subjective. This is why brands usually run their new packaging through rigorous consumer testing to make sure the numbers add up.[46]

185. Brands don't normally launch a new packaging redesign without simultaneously launching a corresponding advertising campaign. This can make the success of the package redesign difficult to measure. You may have a great package redesign that was accompanied by a bad advertising campaign, or you may have a bad package redesign that was accompanied by a good advertising campaign. In both these cases you don't know how the consumers are going to react.[46]

186. When refreshing your brand image, this normally doesn't mean a radical departure from your already existing product design; it usually involves updating the photography used on the packaging and reorganizing the information that is already included on the packaging. You want the product to appear new so it attracts new consumers without scaring your already loyal customers with a packaging they no longer recognize, thinking that their favorite brand has completely changed.

Larger brands generally want increased visibility without compromising the brand identity they worked so hard to build. They want their packaging refreshed in such a way that it attracts new clients without losing the consumers who are already loyal to them.[46]

187. Modifying the package design is no small matter, typical product redesigns can take upwards of three months to do.[46]

188. Large brands may refresh their packaging every two to three years. Startups and small businesses generally need their brand identity (re)created from scratch, and this can happen every 10 years. Their budget is also limited so the work agencies do for small businesses is critical![46]

189. Sometimes in the normal course of business some brands create a new format or change the size of their products (example: when Coca-Cola introduced the mini 7.5 ounce Coca-Cola version of their standard 12 ounce cans.) This means that new packaging has to be made to accommodate the larger or smaller product sizes or to cater to the constraints or demands of their new supplier.[46]

190. Smaller businesses cannot and should not use the same packaging branding design strategy as big brands. If you're a new company, your top priority is visibility.[46]

191. Industries in which all packaging design is nearly identical (the box dimensions or sizes) is likely due to supplier limitations or governmental regulations, or maybe that all of the 'competing' products are actually owned by the same parent company who finds it more economical to print a universal box for all their products. Whatever it may be, if you can differentiate your brand with packaging design, you should by all means.

However if your packaging cannot be redesigned to be distinguished from your competitors, then you'll have to differentiate yourself in other ways.[46]

192. Product and packaging design influence price. Your product might sell for $10 today. Now imagine investing in a design so beautiful and remarkable that you could charge $15 or even $30 for the same product. That profit goes directly to your bottom line. That is the power of visual identity.[58]

193. You need packaging that matches your price; otherwise you will fail because consumers will notice the incongruence.[51]

194. Your typography, color scheme and logo opens or closes your creative possibilities you have at your disposal. Choose them wisely and everything else will come more easily.[58]

195. If you're launching a new product that is aimed at a specific consumer demographic, then you need to design the packaging and supporting advertising for that group of consumers.[60]

196. You do need a strong packaging design and a strong advertising presence. But must you divide your budget between the two? What if you invested your entire budget in creating a product and packaging design so remarkable and strong that it could be the focus of your advertising campaign?[58]

CONSUMERS AND POTENTIAL CUSTOMERS

197. The consumer is more clever and open-minded than you would believe.[17]

198. Be genuine and be in it to help people and you will be successful. Every meeting you have with a consumer is an opportunity for you to bring value.

Always ask yourself this question *"What's in it for them?"* It isn't about you.[22]

199. Begin the persistent ongoing work of being public, and showing people how you can help them. Announce it every day or week, instead of all at once at the start. Your start is not their start. Consumers need many reminders before they'll actually take the time to check you out.[59]

200. What the consumer says they want, and what the consumer actually wants isn't always the same thing. People don't always know what they want. What they think is the problem may not be the problem at all, rather the symptom of another problem.

Never react too quickly, and don't take too much at face value: what people say to you and about you, and request from you. Very often you could be wrong. People may say things to you that you strongly disagree with. So think instead about why they said what they said and resist the temptation to respond with a knee-jerk reaction; you may understand the background behind the response better. Listen to people carefully and you can very often detect underlying reasons for things that aren't overtly said. The more you shut up, the better you become as a listener.[2]

201. Your success is directly related to the tonality of your message. Speak to your consumer as who they want to be, not who they are now.[35]

202. The reasons for which a customer chose to do business with you aren't always the reasons you think. Always keep your ears open and listen to your consumers, understand the way they operate, and how you fit in. [28]

203. You're losing your audience if you're unable to deliver a clear approach. It's really easy to lose 90% of the people who are listening to you. For example, you could have the best content in the world, but with an ugly website, people will leave your website because it's ugly.[7]

204. The internet is an overwhelming infinite of information, but most people tend to be creatures of habit: going to the same newspapers and the same sources to keep an eye on things and to stay up-to-date.[36]

205. Your brand is not what you think your brand is, it is what they (your client/customer) think it is. In the age of social media, you don't tell people what you are; they tell you what you should be.[22]

206. Most of the time, within the first few video frames consumers have already decided whether or not they will share your video. So you really need to provoke an emotional response very quickly.[39]

207. E-reputation dictates that if a person discovers and shares something interesting, then that person feels like a god on the internet. Further, if that person's social network likes what that person shared, it's social proof and means that that person has good taste and is somebody who finds and identifies interesting things, which means that that person will receive more followers.[39]

208. A huge amount of human behavior is devised to minimize transaction costs. To anybody under 30 years old, it might seem weird to call up and physically book an appointment when this could be more conveniently done by app or by web.[44]

209. Be as transparent with people as you can about who you are, what you're doing and how you plan to improve their lives in some incremental way in exchange for their money.[43]

210. When running analytics for your website, don't get discouraged if you aren't getting thousands of visitors per month. Many companies spend money on advertising thinking solely about generating the highest volume of visits and as many immediate conversions as possible. Quantity improves the probability of conversion, but more visitors doesn't necessarily mean more reliable analytics. Quantity actually isn't necessary to conduct quality analytics. The knowledge you can obtain from just 80 relevant visitors who find your website through relevant channels and who convert (purchase, sign-up, share, comment...) is much more important than from 1,000 visitors who don't purchase.[40]

211. Most consumers don't make purchases on their first visit, but instead return to your site multiple times before finally deciding to purchase.[40]

212. When you begin receiving 1,000s of visitors who aren't 'converting,' begin researching in-depth where each and every visitor is coming from because you're probably looking at one of two major problems:

a. The visitors coming to your website aren't people who care about what you offer, in which case you should either begin offering content relevant to these visitors or re-focus your attention to drawing visitors more interested in what you offer.

b. The visitors coming to your website are people who care about what you offer, but something about your website is turning them away, in which case you should re-examine the design, text, content, purchase model, etc.[40]

213. Consumers can all see when a website is too slow, is intrinsically non-ergonomic, or is sketchy and can't be trusted. You might have a website that has an A+ in terms of website functionality to content, except that your website's design makes you look like you're running a phishing scam.[41]

214. Humans can be:

a. Ecologically rational - their behavior may actually be a perfectly sensible course of action given the circumstances in which a person finds him or herself in.

b. Socially rational, or evolutionary rational - a certain degree of copying in our behavior where when in doubt our impulsive instinct to copy the behavior of others is essential to becoming a social species.[44]

215. In addition to being taught, one of the ways consumers learn is actually seeing how other people do things and then assuming there's a reason for them doing it.[44]

216. Behavioral economics can be useful to small businesses because it reveals very small things you

can in your spare time. Some of which require no budget at all which can really make a big difference.[44]

217. People are starving for good content, and are willing to accept unoriginal stuff just to fill their docket – just to fulfill their online posting calendar and keep their website fresh.[20]

218. Everyone hates spam, yet they continue to give brands their personal information and agree to the terms and conditions that allow their information to be sold to third parties. That's why brands always provide an added interest - such as contests and giveaways to entice you to give them your personal information.

There are tools out there that allow consumers to unsubscribe from brand mailings with just the click of a button, but in many cases people may forget that they unsubscribed from a website or a brands newsletter just a week prior and then re-subscribe to that brands newsletter again.[52]

219. Location is important to branding. When consumers go shopping they choose to shop at places based on price range.[51]

220. There's a difference in the way customers perceive sales people. In the 1980's there were classes to learn how to "close a deal." It was like robotic sales with people reading from a script. Since then there's been a huge shift. Now it's all about relationship. You first must learn to like and trust people, then comes the business.[22]

221. Listening is extremely hard. Until you understand your category through the perspective of your consumer, you have very little understanding about your brand or product.[55]

222. Consumers have to be able to recognize themselves in your advertising.[53]

223. Until you have a bad review, people don't take what you do or claim too seriously. Once people start saying you aren't perfect, that's when people start taking notice of you.[56]

224. The more early adopters talk about you, the more people take that early adopter's advice and use it themselves.[50]

225. If users make a mistake it will most likely be within the first five minutes of downloading your app (or product) while they're deciding whether or not to trust and use you, and so you'll instantly have negative feedback going on there.[50]

226. Usually your brain makes the decision for you as to how you see an entity; it chooses the pictures you are going to remember or consciously perceive and at the same time lets you overlook others.[54]

WEBSITE DESIGN & USER EXPERIENCE (UX)

227. If your blog requires serious interaction with your main website such as blog posts that allow for one-click shopping, then using the same content management system (CMS) makes integration easier.[41]

228. It's important to remember that many of the free services available today: unlimited email, games, books, movies, software programs, etc. are free THANKS TO the paid banner advertising around them - the brand has included revenue generated from banner advertising in their business model so that they can offer their products/services to you. This means consumers must make an important distinction between annoying banner advertisements and brands that plaster their websites with banner advertising.[38]

229. Websites and templates should look minimalist and simple to put together, but that doesn't mean the template was easy to put together and easy to just make major modifications to as you want to and on a whim.[41]

230. A lot of websites that host guest bloggers have rules limiting promotion down to only a two-line biography included with the post. This means you're writing about things that are relevant and not overtly promotional.[29]

231. Adding something to a website can be easy, but perhaps at the direct cost of functionality.[41]

232. Think about the entry points that hackers use:

    a. Exploiting text input. Every place on your website where people input text is a potential open hole for hackers. If your website only displays images, text and video, then there's no way hackers can hack into your website unless it's through your FTP or your hosting service.
    b. Exploiting your hosting service. You're at the mercy of your hosting service's security

competencies. All of the major services are usually very secure.

c. Cracking your passwords. Choose strong passwords. Upper and lower case with numbers and symbols.

d. Exploiting your dedicated server. If you're using a dedicated server, make sure you've got a good server administrator, a Linux or Unix administrator.

e. Exploiting outdated CMS versions. Once you start using one, make sure you're up-to-date on the latest versions.

f. Exploiting your computer. Your computer itself could be weak, providing a portal for hackers. If hackers get into your computer where you store your passwords and confidential information, they have your website.[41]

233. Make good content. Tactics to optimize SEO are so readily available and are built into the major CMSs. Make good content and the rest will follow.[41]

234. Google's algorithm is like a voting system, and every link is considered a vote. But not all votes are equal: higher PageRanked websites have more heavily weighted votes. From a selfish point of view, blogrolls and link sharing are a bad idea. If you want to be number one, you want a lot of people linking to you and you want to link to very few.[41]

235. Set SMART goals (Specific, Measurable, Acceptable, Realistic, and Time-bound).[40]

236. There are 3 pillars for the base of your website:

a. **Acquisition**:

- Where are your visitors coming from?

- Which source they are coming from?
- Which landing page are they arriving on?
- What is the bounce rate for each of those landing pages?

b. **Conversion:**

- What is the conversion rate of your registration and/or checkout form?
- What is the behavior of your visitors prior to purchase?

c. **Loyalty**:

- How do you retain your visitors and convince them to purchase?
- What is your customer relationship management (CRM) strategy?[40]

237. Ten things to evaluate when testing your website:

a. **Visit site for first impressions.** Begin by visiting your website and noting down the general impression you get from it.

- What is the objective of your website? To sell a product/service, inform, gather data…?
- Can you immediately understand what you can do on your website?
- Are your 'Calls to action' obvious?
- Are the steps needed to "convert" (purchase or sign-up) easy to understand and navigate? Is the check-out process short and simple?
- Is your website organized and its ergonomics clear?
- Are your FAQ page, product issues, and return policies clear?

Test your website's search bar (if you have one) to see how well it works and what kind of results it gives you.

How consumers search Google to find what they're looking for is very different from how they would search on your individual website's search bar. Tracking how people search on your website's search bar gives you a clue to the kind of visitors you're attracting and what is of interest to them. If the keywords your visitors are searching for are not what your website is about, then either your attracting the wrong people or your readers are telling you what you should be writing about.

b. **Determine your acquisition strategy.** How exactly does your brand attract visitors to your website - via paid Google searches? Social media platforms? Other?

Determine your top 10 or so landing pages and track every channel through which your visitors find you - no matter how miniscule. Track it to find its origin. It might be a blog post comment you or somebody linked to from years before, or it might very well lead to an undiscovered community of people you didn't even know existed.

If you find that 90% of your traffic is coming from Facebook, then what would you do if Facebook's next policy change tampers with your traffic flow? If Google search (paid and organic) makes up 90% of your traffic, then what are you going to do if a financially backed competitor purchases your keywords and steals your traffic? Don't put all of your eggs in one basket, keep a diverse portfolio of incoming traffic sources. It's much safer for the success of your website.

Your acquisition strategy should be as balanced as possible - paid search, organic search, social media traffic, emailing campaigns, etc.

c. **Perform quick fixes and maintenance.** After you've ensured your acquisition strategy is solid. Check what you can fix quickly and easily: your top landing pages - your most popular entrance pages. Check your landing page's bounce rates. If your bounce rate is up to 50%, then there is surely something wrong. It could be 2 things:

- Your leading the wrong people to your website, or
- Your landing page itself is not efficient and not optimized.

d. **Conduct website's keywords analysis.** Begin primarily with visitor loyalty in the last month:

- How long did they stay on your website?
- How many pages did they visit?
- How frequently do they come back?

Compare search engine management (SEM) with bounce rate with the cost of running and maintaining your channel to determine the channel's profitability.

e. **Conduct a comprehensive content visibility analysis.** Determine which sections of your website are the most visited and which content is the most consumed and visible on the internet, and return to step c (perform quick fixes and maintenance) to improve them.

f. **Examine your 'Call to Action.'** Visitors are very wary about making purchases from strangers. So you have to push and prod and reassure them and convince them it's simple, fast, safe, and moreover that the product/service they are purchasing will have value for them. Assess:

    • How are your unique selling points (USP) presented?
    • What call to action (CTA) buttons are used?
    • How relevant are those CTA buttons?
    • Where are the buttons located on your website?
    • Are there reassurance factors such as Paypal verified, security and membership logos?

g. **Examine customer loyalty.** Begin primarily with visitor loyalty: How long do visitors stay on your website, how many pages do they visit, and how frequently do the visitors return to your website.

    Next examine the follow-up email after the consumer has converted:

    • What does the email say?
    • Does it motivate the consumer to discover your brand's YouTube channel, blog, special blog posts, other products and services available?
    • Does it take the consumer's hand and help him/her discover your brand?

h. **Conduct ongoing CRM quality analysis.** Look deeply into your website's analytics. Browse through your email history to see what emails have been sent, how often, and what has been communicated in them.

i. **Monitor customer lifetime value.** Over time, some clients can have much more value if they purchase with a high frequency or a high average cart value. It is important that you identify who they are and where they come from to leverage the right actions to make them more loyal.

Three questions you should remember:

- How does your brand exalt and focus on loyal consumers who generate the most money?
- How does your brand entice consumers to purchase more?
- How does your brand deepen the relationship and make consumers more loyal?

j. **Analyze your customer loyalty retention strategy.** Work with business intelligence team(s) to join analytics with your brand's database to identify consumer profiles to determine who has the highest risk of abandoning your brand, marking your brand's emails as spam, or being enticed to a competitor.

- Which conversion path do consumers follow the most?
- Which menu bar button(s) do consumers click on the most?

- Which video(s) do consumers play the most and for how long they watch them?
- How can you rearrange your website to improve/optimize performance all the way down to your CTA buttons?[40]

238. Put as much content as you can on your home page without overcrowding it, and organize your navigation and website to reduce the total number of clicks visitors must make to find any piece of information they want to as few as possible. The more clicks visitors must make, the more likely they are to leave.[32]

239. For a digital campaign to run smoothly you need all the right resources including strategists, site architects, web designers and good coders. Nowadays anyone can create lovely pre-made templates for blogs, but if you want a stunningly beautiful website that is correctly SEO'ed, draws visitors in and converts them, that won't break or get hacked, then it's going to take a professional to code it.[27]

240. Content management systems (CMS) and services are constantly improving, and it can be expensive and time consuming to switch platforms, especially if you have +1,000s of pages with 10,000s of links (internal and external). Therefore companies generally budget for a modernization of their already existing site.[32]

241. The purpose of social media should be so that visitors can follow you and interact with you, and many blogs try to accomplish this by linking to their social media platforms using a simple hyperlinked icon. But sending your visitors away from your website and toward social media platforms before you've had a chance to 'convert' them is extremely dangerous from a Customer Relations Management (CRM) perspective because, let's face it, Facebook and Twitter are professionals at occupying, distracting, and engaging their users. Sending your visitors to them could lead to them getting swept away onto other pages and websites before they've had a chance to 'follow' you.[32]

A better approach would be using application programming interfaces (API) integration between your website and social media platforms so visitors can immediately follow you without having to leave your website. Why send your visitors away from your website to your Facebook page when you could integrate Facebook directly into your website? When you think about it this way, your website is no longer a free standing website with share buttons, but part of a bigger online eco-system, like a dashboard your visitors can follow you and share your content again and **again** with just one click and without having to leave your website.[32]

Be careful though! Using API requires a certain budget and you must stay on top of it. API policies and software do change, so there's always a risk you spend a sizeable chunk of money integrating an awesome API into your website only to find at the next policy change or update that it no longer works as effectively as it did, or that a better tool has been launched. Expired widgets, tools, and API versions make websites appear outdated, unprofessional and abandoned.[32]

242. Because the digital world is so fluid - a constantly shifting landscape - it's easy to be misconstrued as being instant and even disposable. It's far easier to take down a website than to pull a major outdoor campaign which is already live.[27]

243. Having to tell a developer - who's maybe 90% of the way through a complex site or app build - that you're changing something quite fundamental in the project is an inevitable reality in such a constantly shifting landscape. This is why it is imperative to take the time to thoroughly understand your needs at the beginning of your project.[27]

244. The days of digital being a complete afterthought - a bookend to major campaigns - are over. If you incorporate a digital component into a TV or print campaign late in the project, it will show. For a solid 360 approach, digital needs to be a part of the plan from the outset and accompany print and TV ads. This is something brands are incorporating more and more into their branding strategy.[27]

245. In the deadline driven momentum of *'we have to get our website up NOW!,'* some brands don't honor themselves in the right way and are rushed. They don't build their website with as much care as they took in building their brand. This is unfortunate because when digital isn't executed well, consumers can see it right away. So elevating your online presence to become a real and compelling part of the brand experience should hopefully become the universal goal. Even with the timeline of getting your website and digital experiences up and running, everything should be as beautiful and meaningful as you can make it.[26]

246. Don't just look at SEO as a way of improving your online search rank. Not so much adapting your website to the way search engines work, but as you go through the process of doing your SEO you'll find you improve the way you present your company and talk about it. It forces you to define what you are, who you are, what you do, and how you do it. The whole process of SEO forces you to improve your own view and marketing of your product or service.[28]

247. If when people go to your site they don't know what it does or why they should use it, or if you're having problems with growth because people aren't being retained (or converted via signing up or purchasing), take another look at your product and it's presentation.[50]

248. Responsive design is a website design that can work on every computer device from smart phones to tablets to desktops. Many clients believe that making a website responsive is as easy as adding a line or two of code to the html. But each different device requires a different website design to be made. Buying a responsive website design isn't just buying one website design; it's buying several website designs.[52]

249. Consumers tend to assume that when a digital product (website, application...) doesn't work, it's the brand's fault. It could be the consumer's internet connection or your website's host are experiencing technical difficulties. The end consumer may be right to some extent to think this way because it makes it easier for them to distinguish brands who care about their image, plus it keeps brands on their toes and forces them to continually raise the bar and improve their products and services and ensure that they are better than their competitor's.[52]

250. Some applications and websites are trying to go viral and facilitate exposure. Some go too far by making their product annoying to use, so users are constantly trying to use the product while not posting everything they do onto Facebook. Some brands really go a step too far.[50]

251. Anything can be exploited by a hacker. Most skilled people who design websites nowadays are aware of basic security protocol, so you shouldn't worry about it too much. If a hacker wants to hack your site, it's going to happen.

If you hire a designer you should make it clear that security is a priority for you and make sure that you know what they have done to your site and what sort of security measures they have taken.[50]

252. If you have a very simple product and you've already nailed what your product does, and when people open up your app or visit your website they know exactly what it does and why they need it, then by all means don't spend any more money on user experience (UX) and invest in getting the word out about your product.[50]

253. Don't reinvent the wheel. Chances are whatever service or widget it is that you'd like to incorporate into your website already exists in some form. Before you spend time and money trying to create it, search the internet and see if you can find it.[32]

254. Instead of your homepage being your blog, consider creating a read-only (no comments section) corporate informational page that outlines your philosophy, values, and goals, has your social media API integration, and links to your FAQ page, blog, and press page - Like a dashboard for your website.[32]

255. All other things being correct (your branding strategy, marketing campaign, a desirable product, good copywriting, etc.): If your visitors land on your homepage and are confused about what your product is or why they should use it, then your UX designer has failed.[50]

256. More and more brands today are organizing their websites so that the logo (or title), menu bar, search bar, and social media buttons are on one single 'responsive' bar at the top of the site. Doing so:

   a. Maximizes your 'above the fold' content
   b. Highlights your content, which is the reason people visit your website in the first place
   c. Makes your site more compatible with mobile devices such as iPads and smart phones.[40]

257. Nothing you create should have a cheap look or feel or seem thoughtless; consumers can be very perfectionist when it comes to visual matters. It has nothing to do with luck but rather with a trained, precise view of how things should look like paired with an intuitive knowledge of how things look 'right.' Sometimes it's about how many millimeters a font is separated from an image, no detail is irrelevant and the human eye is ruthless (especially when it's trained).[54]

258. There are some cases where 'forgivable' patterns can definitely be helpful for startups: Web site features that consumers generally dislike however are willing to tolerate, or that consumers accidentally do but have the opportunity to go back and undo if they want – Most people will probably just let it go – up to a certain point.[50]

259. If your objective (of your marketing campaign) is to increase sales, then first and foremost you need to commit to creating an amazing e-commerce site. Make it the best 'selling' experience consumers encounter.[26]

260. If your objective (of your marketing campaign) is to honestly reflect the character of your brand and build a community around your brand, then you have to do the real work to get there.[26]

261. It's one thing to create a functional website, and quite another to design a beautiful website filled with quality content that gets shared.[41]

WEBSITE CONTENT

262. In addition to your marketing efforts across your social media platforms, it might not be necessary to create an individual website for every campaign you do. A sub-domain or maybe even just an individual page on your website or a post on your blog might suffice. It all depends on the goal and life of your advertising campaign.[32]

263. Websites can have high traffic and low PageRank as well as low traffic and a high PageRank. You need to weigh them both to make sure that people are reading your material in addition to the value that you get from doing guest posts on other sites.[29]

264. Consider having a budget for production rather than for advertising. Controlling your social media with good information can be a more useful form of advertising than paying for advertising space.[30]

265. It is the consistent publishing of quality videos, music, and photography that bring people to your website again and again and again. HOWEVER, it is text that brings reputation that photos and videos cannot. Your website, therefore, should contain a healthy balance of all three.[30]

266. A general rule is if you want earned media, you cannot showcase your product; you must deliver interesting and useful content first.[37]

267. At the end of the day your work could very well end up being one television advertisement among 1,000s that nobody you know will ever see.[15]

268. On the internet, consumers can easily spend their day going from one website to another website to another website without end. So the more relevant you make your website and content align with your reader's interests and lifestyle, the more often that person will return to your website as a starting point. Organize your website and offer content to become your target demographics' favorite starting point every time they turn on their computer.[34]

269. When researching for a blog post you are writing, always try to keep a critical eye in everything you write. And as often as possible try to meet the owner(s) and the people in charge because often times there's an interesting story behind how the company or product came into existence. Perhaps they are two people who normally should never have crossed paths, but somehow did and it turned into the brand you're writing about today. You might find that much more interesting than a simple press packet.[24]

270. You've worked so hard getting traffic to your website. You've written high-quality useful articles and/or you've paid for the traffic either through money or through blood, sweat, and tears. Why would you want to send people away via advertising on your site - especially for a commission of a couple of pennies? Ads can be profitable if you have millions of site hits a month. But if you have a smaller blog or website, and especially if you target a niche-market, then it's more profitable for you to sell a product or service. You don't want to send people off your site. You want them on your website for as long as possible until they buy or sign-up.[20]

271. Once your blog gets big enough you'll begin getting requests to sell links. People will contact you willing to pay upwards of $500.00 just to put a specific hyperlink on a specific word on a specific article. If it's relevant and something you're interested in, then why not?[20]

272. If you want to drive traffic to your website, understand that Google has been blocking traditional search and their algorithm changes and evolves often.[16]

273. If you haven't launched your web site/blog yet, wait until you have at least 10 posts ready to publish at the same time before officially launching, rather than just one or two posts. Blogs with just one or two posts can come across as dead or abandoned.[51]

274. There's a big difference between just blogging what you feel like and consciously choosing every image according to its color and what it's depicting.[54]

275. Image copyright issues are a legal grey area that are discussed on a very emotional & far too personal level, especially on the internet. This makes certain people feel like they have to guard over 'their' artwork like watchdogs no matter who approaches it or what is done with it.[54]

276. Do your best to blog as transparently as possible, crediting the original sources and tracing every picture that you find back to its originator.[54]

SOCIAL MEDIA MARKETING

277. For small companies, it's better to focus on and be really efficient in 2-4 main social platforms (relevant to your demographic) than to have 9 different profiles and not have enough time to make them of good quality (inactive).

You can't keep your eye on every conversation on every social platform, so you're taking the risk that people will criticize you without your immediately knowing. Running a social media platform is a full time job in itself, and even community managers aren't available 24/7.[8]

278. For strategic branding to be successful in the long-term, you need to know:

   a. How to use the various social media platforms to collect and analyze data on each platform your brand is represented on
   b. How to make this data relevant to be more attractive for your consumers
   c. How to talk with your consumers using a 1-to-1 strategy.[7]

279. As soon as you have a Facebook fan page, you suddenly have to handle important issues like:

   a. What is my community management style?
   b. What is my conversation calendar?
   c. What is the real value of becoming new fan for the consumer?
   d. How can I distinguish between fans who are merely fans and fans who are also buyers and owners of my product, service, or royalty program?

As soon as you have a fan page, you also have to have a crisis strategy. Because as you're opening a page, you're letting the possibility for everybody and anybody to talk with you, but also to critique or insult you. You need to find a way to be reactive and manage these kinds of situations. Opening a Facebook page and simply posting things isn't a safe solution.[7]

280. It's really difficult to have a consolidated view of your market. If you're a brand and you have 20 platforms, it's not impossible, but it's difficult to have a consumer-centric view.

It's also very important NOT to have a vertical

strategy for each social media platform, but to link them all together. If you're going to have that many platforms, you're going to need an approach to help you organize all your data into one easy-to-read location so you can collect and analyze the data from the different social media platforms.[7]

281. Some brands think in terms of channels and not content. You 'need' a Facebook page but don't know what to do with it. You 'need' a website but don't know where you want to go with it.

Without a goal and a clearly defined brand objective there's no reason for you to be on Facebook, or any social network for that matter. Diving headlong into a social media platform without thoroughly thinking it through could backfire and you could regret it.[32]

282. In online communities, spammers eventually start becoming a problem, and then a daily annoyance. Your community itself should be able to weed out the spammers.[57]

283. Put your community members first. There could be a few occasions where you'll have to tell friends to STOP doing something, and even banned friends or people you like because they are causing more damage to your community spirit than good.[57]

284. Respect other groups and admins. Don't go spamming your community onto other groups or they will treat you as spam and block you. If instead you contact the admin privately and request to post in their community, often times they'll actively use their influence and help promote you. You can return the favor for them and both of your communities benefit. After all everyone started with an idea, and so long as your idea doesn't compete with existing or future projects there is no reason not to help someone who approaches you correctly.[57]

285. By actively managing your communities you can clearly recognize the same recurring issues, problems and challenges from members.[57]

286. It's important that your target audience isn't following you or your brand; but that they are following the community.

The beauty of creating a community around the group and not around your brand is that the community supports itself and provides its own content and you can merely monitor it to keep the spammers at bay. If you were to walk away from your community tomorrow, it should potentially be able to continue by itself indefinitely.[57]

CUSTOMER RELATIONSHIP MANAGEMENT (CRM)

287. Success relies on the quality of relationships you build.[22]

288. Customer focused marketing, which is different from trying to win new customers, it trying to develop and create stronger relationships with existing brand consumers.[35]

289. When you work on CRM strategy, your main issues are developing your relationship with your clients so that your clients increase their consumption with your brand - that they visit, buy, and use your product or service more and more. CRM is loyalty.[35]

290. Loyal brand users have different needs and communication demands than non-loyal users who you want to convince to use your brand.[35]

291. You can't just open a Facebook page for consumers and then call it a CRM campaign because you can't identify loyal users from people who just clicked the 'like' button. There's no way to distinguish nor reward.[35]

292. When you develop a relational website, you use analytics and other metrics to track your user's behavior on your website. Monitoring your user's behavior is relatively easy if it is a commercial website because if you change something and can see the difference fairly quickly - more sales, less sales.[35]

293. With advertising, once the advertising stops, the traffic stops. With CRM, once you get an email address and create customer loyalty, your reach is unlimited.[35]

294. In the long run, maintaining a CRM budget is less expensive than an advertising budget. It's less expensive to keep a client than it is to win a new client.[35]

295. When a brand enters a subscription-based market as a new player, their advertising budget is poured into winning clients and market share and stealing clients from the established players. But this won't be easy because for customers to switch they have to cancel their existing contracts, which means losing their fidelity points with their current provider. But once the brand establishes their database, they can scale back on their advertising budget and focus on CRM campaigns to create loyal customers.[35]

296. For newsletters sent to your loyal consumers who have voluntarily given you their email address and opted-in to receive it, a good open rate and click-through rate would be between 15-20%. This guarantees a steady stream of traffic to your website.[35]

297. Your main objective of a CRM campaign is to capture information about your visitors which you can then use to better meet their needs. This is best done through interaction. Everything about your CRM website should be designed to create a community and draw your consumers into your brand. Create a lifestyle around your brand.[35]

298. Advertising is a mass media approach, whereas CRM is a personalized approach. You have to know precisely who your consumers are, their needs, their behavior, and with this data you can develop a very personalized approach to engage in a relationship.[35]

299. There are always discriminating demographic facts that separate one demographic from another. You just have to know how to identify and then act on them.[35]

300. Build your database. To do this you must get people to follow you on social media or give you their email

address. To get information from people you must peak their curiosity and convince them to give it to you.[35]

301. Require an email address to sign up and then email confirmation before a person can 'see what is on the other side.' Out of curiosity, people may sign up for your service but might not see its worth or don't get involved. But perhaps 3, 5, 9 months later they'll receive an email from you, and then all of the sudden they see your product or service's worth and become loyal users.[35]

302. If you don't have a consumer database there is no CRM. If you don't have marketing campaign tools there is no possibility of CRM because you can't industrialize the content you send and personalize your campaign. CRM campaigns do require a big budget upfront.[35]

303. CRM doesn't give immediate and measureable results like banner advertising on the internet would. CRM campaigns take time to develop and the return-on-investment isn't evident until the long run.[35]

304. One of the great things about direct marketing is that it's scalable. The simple thinking behind direct marketing embraces universal principles such as *"the best source of customers is your past customers."* Those can be applied to any business, large or small. Therefore, you should ask yourself *"What can I do to get people to come back?"* Because it's much easier to retain a customer than it is to acquire one. That's useful to a small business just as much as to a large one.[44]

305. Understand that it can sometimes take several months and multiple visits before a prospect actually becomes interested in your product/service and goes to the *"I buy"* step. Only paying attention to the surface level measurements of direct conversion rate and profitability of their media campaigns could actually be holding your business back.

For example, consider during the Christmas season you spend $10 advertising to customer X and $30 advertising to customer Y, and after the Christmas season your conversion rate and profitability measurements tell you that customer X spent $20 and customer Y spent $25.

If you stop only at these surface-level analytics, you'll be tempted to jump to the conclusion that customer X is more profitable than customer Y, and so you should focus your advertising budget on customer X.

But if you dig deeper into your analytics, looking at the rest of the year, you might learn that customer X's $20 purchase was just a one-time purchase, while customer Y returned and made two more purchases, generating over $100 in revenue, thus making customer Y the bigger spender.[40]

306. CRM begins at the subscription form. It's important that the form be short, simple, clear. Built into your subscription form you should remind the visitor of all the assets and reasons to subscribe to your website, for example say by subscribing clients receive special promotions, privileges, coupons, gifts, etc.[40]

307. Networking is a full-time job in itself. Spend four hours a day seven days a week building your social media profiles, commenting on photos, answering emails and responding to comments. It's extremely important because it's how you stay close to your readers. It's not complicated to see when you look at your analytics and see that you have 2,500 people visiting your website and 800 of them have shared or are leaving comments. [24]

308. When things don't go as planned, make sure you do an even better job. Customers don't care about *"how you feel"* or *"circumstances beyond your control."* You want to be at your best at that moment because otherwise you'll have a handful of unsatisfied customers feeding off of each other. [56]

ADVERTISING

309. The higher up in the company you move the farther away from the creative process you are and the more administrative responsibilities you have. When you're further away from the campaign, you manage many creative briefs at the same time, and you must keep the client in mind. [17]

310. Sometimes someone who isn't used to working in communication - a person educated and with a strong background in engineering or banking, for example, moves into advertising. Of course that person will not be at ease. What makes the difference is *"Does this person have enough sensibility; is this person able enough to think like a consumer?"* [17]

311. Assuming a 2% conversion rate, for every 100 visitors you'll get two conversions (people who purchase your $10.00 product/service). $10.00 x 2 = $20.00. So 100 visitors = $20.00. So don't spend more than $20.00 on advertising to get 100 visitors. It's simple, but that means you have to do your research and know your variables.[20]

312. If you have an advertising budget and no product, then write free content and invest your advertising budget into creating a product to sell.[20]

313. Creative marketing seems always to be chasing its own tail, because you always have to be more creative than the next guy to stand out from the crowd of messages.[20]

314. It's expensive to buy media; it's expensive to generate compelling creative material. So the next best thing, maybe even a better way to do this, is to provide a lot of value for people. And you do that through content.[20]

315. The everyday mundane paperwork of keeping your schedule planning accurate and up-to-date is very important for the profitability of an advertising campaign as well as the future of your company. This is because this information allows you to monitor all your expenses and time spent. Financial controllers work with this information every day, and many financial reports that companies use to make strategic decisions have precise deadlines, and thus rely heavily on this information being accurate.[9]

316. When pitching to a client, or when preparing for your own advertising project, prepare a VERY detailed project outline. It's safer for you to put a lot of details of what you're offering because if the client later wants something additional you can show them what you originally agreed upon and that what they want isn't included in the originally agreed upon deal.[9]

317. Clients rightly want to make sure they get what they paid for and they may even want to take an active role in the development of their advertising campaign. But it's a mistake to think that anyone can do advertising, and clients must learn to trust the agency more.[8]

318. An important factor in evaluating the worth of an advertising campaign is on the amount of time necessary to complete the project. If you allot 10 hours for a project and you complete it in 5 hours, that's great. But if it takes you 20 hours, then you'll have lost time and money on the project.[9]

319. Focus on one to two objectives at a time, with all actions responding to these essential objectives. If you have multiple objectives, your advertising efforts won't be as effective. One to two objectives max.[14]

320. Just because an advertising campaign works in one country with one demographic and culture doesn't mean it will work in another. You have to adjust your objective, your budget, and key performance indicators (KPI) such as impressions, clicks, click-through rate, bounce rate, # of completed goals, conversion rate, sales, return on investment...

according to the demographic/market you're expanding to. Make sure you know your market.[3]

321. People unfamiliar with an advertiser's job might think it's quite simple and superficial and not take the agency's role as seriously as they should. This is because people don't see all the work that goes on behind the scenes in creating a campaign. People know advertising can be expensive and time-consuming, but many times they don't appreciate the cost behind the action.[4]

322. Data is the future of advertising. If you understand the importance of and utilize data collection, treatment and how to incorporate it into your branding strategy, then you have a strong chance of becoming a leader in the next few years.[7]

323. Advertising is a lot of work and everything seems to be extremely and equally important. With advertising, you can have the feeling that the reputation and future of your brand is riding on this ad campaign, which is true up to a point. But usually it's the mountain that gives birth to the mouse. Everything could seem dramatic and important, but you must stay in control and calm. After all, it's just advertising.[33]

324. There's no perfect recipe, but it starts with a strong creative brief and a very involved creative team.[33]

325. When clients say during the pre-production meeting (PPM) *"We'll handle that problem in post-production,"* you can be certain you're going to have big problems during the post-production. Don't end your PPM until ALL of your problems have been solved and agreed upon. If you don't, then problems will only get bigger and bigger, and more costly.[33]

326. People can be led to think that creative advertising is very easy and you can create beautiful and stunning images with only a computer. But this demands expertise, time, and the talent of people involved.[6]

If the creative is really talented then the rough mock-ups will look really great. But don't confuse a mock-up with a final product. *"The mock-up is perfect, so why do we need to spend more money and do more? Let's just use these?"*

Mock-ups need to be developed because:

a. The mock-ups are fictive.
b. We don't own the copyright to the images used, so we have to create our own.
c. Mock-ups look beautiful in double A4 size because they're small. But the larger you make the photo, the more pixels are used, and the more detail and definition are lost.
d. Research must be conducted to validate the idea and verify that it doesn't exist elsewhere to avoid legal problems in the future.[6]

327. Writing an ad that works across the entire US is like trying to write an ad that works just as well in London, Greece and parts of Russia.[27]

328. Typical problems advertising campaigns run into include:

a. Budgeting problems

b. Internal or relationship problems - a typical advertising project changes hands many times between the creative brief to the final product. People have different deadlines and ways of working and we must not lose sight of the initial purpose

c. Equipment & materials - Making sure everyone has exactly what they need to do their part of the campaign correctly[39]

329. If you're a blogger or a small business looking to get more traffic to your website, then advertising isn't the way to go. The online landscape is changing - people don't click on ads, and they don't like being advertised to, so you have to learn to do it in a lot more subtle ways. Fortunately there are many free ways to get your name out there that just require time and a little bit of knowledge.[29]

330. With digital experiences you can't taste or smell or touch, so there is something compelling about printed matter where brands can appeal to the consumer's sense of touch and the nuance of how something is printed - the smell of ink and paper, the sound, the sensuality of it seems more intimate.[26]

331. At the first presentation brands may love what agencies come up with, but as they move together through the stages of the project, some brands may decide that the project is perhaps a little too ambitious and risky and/or won't fit with their consumers. As a result the campaign turns into a classical, smaller brand activation.[61]

332. It can be challenging because you can get clients who only want to attain a short-term goal. Some clients may only have one point of contact with the ad agency, but usually there are two or three people. Even if there is only one person on the client's marketing team who initially isn't concerned with getting to the deeper meaning of the brand, when agencies show them the thinking behind the ideas, their peers really come to our support and really do their own best job to sell the ideas internally to their teams. When it touches somebody they become an advocate within their company.[26]

333. Brands may be scared that agencies are pushing the brand to be too risky solely for the agency to win awards, and not for the brand to increase sales and exposure. This has led to a certain apprehension with advertisers, and why if an idea is 'too' creative for the brand, they have a tendency to outright refuse the idea instead of trying to understand why it would be in their best interest to be different and stand out from their competition.[45]

334. Quality agencies want the best for their clients; not only to win awards. But agencies also need to win awards because brands want to work with award-winning agencies.[42]

335. If you take out an ad on a subway, you might get a few people to check you out, but it will be in a vacuum.[50]

336. An ever-expanding accessibility to improving software such as Photoshop and InDesign as well as an increase in the general population's ability to use said software has led many people to believe that anybody can do advertising. This belief has caused advertising agencies to lose power.[45]

337. The once expensive software used by professionals has become more affordable to the ordinary person who lacks the creative training and experience to consistently come up with strong ideas and turn them into effective advertising campaigns. Just because you've learned how to use the software doesn't mean you can build functional architecture. It's the ability to <u>consistently</u> come up with strong ideas that makes the professional's craft so necessary.[47]

338. Consumers tend to have a bad opinion about advertising, mostly because the great majority of the advertising they're exposed to nowadays isn't very good.[47]

339. Many brands with big advertising budgets invest in saturating the consumer's field of perception, be it in books, on television, or in the metro. This makes it easy for consumers to come to the conclusion that all advertising is bad when bad or mediocre advertising is all they see.[47]

340. Clients often impose constraints that agencies must abide by. Some constraints can be constructive and actually help in the idea brainstorming process such as a budget or time limitation, but sometimes those constraints are very subjective; for example: *'You can't use blue.'* This is the part of the job that advertisers don't really learn at school.[45]

341. At the end of the day your finished work could very well end up being one television advertisement among 1,000s that nobody you know will ever see.[15]

342. People don't realize just how manipulative marketing is. Hypnosis techniques dramatically improve results.[16]

343. Sometimes one project can accomplish multiple objectives, but it can't accomplish everything: increase sales, have better communication, be present on all social media platforms... and on a small budget.[8]

344. You cannot have one source for inspiration, you must have many exchanges. The people you follow on your social media profiles share things with you and give you ideas. The people you associate with determine your level of creativity. Don't necessarily narrow down the people you follow, expand; choose wisely and meet as many people as possible.[13]

345. Smart advertising is becoming less about interruption and more about providing quality content and experience.[38]

346. Your advertisement must touch a definable emotion: funny or sad, etc. Because advertisements have such a short amount of time in front of the consumer's eyes, every advertisement you create must:

    a. Capture the consumer's attention
    b. Surprise the consumer with something funny, happy, sad, scary...[53]

347. Advertising boils down to two elements: form and content.

    a. **Form:** If you make a list of every advertising technique used throughout the ages, certain patterns will emerge. You could then theoretically apply those same techniques to your brand and come up with a list of effective advertising campaign ideas which would 'statistically' give you a higher guaranteed chance of success.

b. **Content:** The content refers to the experiences, observations, and insights that you apply to the form. Having content involves constantly exposing yourself to new and fresh things in the world. The content you have in your head will only be as new and fresh and powerful as the ideas and experiences you expose yourself to. Your content comes from both inside the world of advertising, but more importantly outside of the world of advertising.

First learn all the techniques (form), and then play with the ideas (content).[53]

348. It is possible that a product packaging redesign can save a failing brand, but you cannot bet the future of your business on making your packaging different or more appealing hoping it will be enough.

Advertising does need to be a part of your branding strategy so that by the time consumers find themselves in that 'moment of truth' situation at the point of purchase with what consumers always buy in hand and your product in the other; they have already had at least some prior experience with your brand.[46]

349. People love good advertising. When people see advertising they like, the first thing they want to do is share it with everyone they know.[47]

350. If you approach banner advertising as a branding campaign – a way of getting your logo in front of a large audience of consumers, then banner advertising can be considered a success. However as a branding campaign it can be difficult to rate your results because while you can tell how many impressions your banner received, you don't know who actually noticed your banners and read the message on it.[52]

351. As a creative it's your job to discover, and you can't do your job if you aren't exposing yourself to new things. It's impossible. And you won't discover things if you're only watching television and looking in places where already discovered things are just hitting mainstream.[39]

352. It can happen that during the creative process the central objective(s) outlined in your creative brief can be forgotten, which could cause the final project to go off rail. The strategic planners' job is to inspire outstanding campaigns while acting as a truth-keeper, so in a perfect world strategic planners are involved in every step of your campaign process.[42]

353. Don't be a Google planner. Good and specific insight isn't always obtained from behind a desk or in front of a computer. The irony of this is that most of the time you are behind your desk and in front of your computer.[42]

354. Brands that budget for banner advertising see it as an opportunity for consumers to click on the banner and directly access their website. Banner ads usually promote offers and can be a great way to increase sales. As long as 'enough' consumers click on the banner advertising to show a justifiable return on investment, brands will continue to devote a certain budget to it.[52]

355. Advertising is often there just as a reminder and to say *'Hello, we still exist;'* advertising is the last thing you do when you launch a product.[51]

356. As a rule of thumb for large companies with huge budgets, spend around 10% of your budget creating and producing your idea – creating flyers or videos, etc. The rest of your budget should go towards buying advertising space.[51]

357. There will be a certain amount of loss in any campaign, and you must accept this. No marketing campaign can ever be 100% successful. Ultimately, is there a return on investment? Are you getting more money back from the money you are spending into your campaigns?[52]

358. Advertise parity products by helping consumers see a difference.[53]

359. Creativity is an everyday job. You can't think in terms of *"I'm going to take this idea from an exposition I saw and use it for my next advertising campaign."* Keep particularly striking ideas in an organized folder near your desk. You may not use it now, but you know it will be a source of inspiration somewhere down the line.[53]

360. It's important to nourish yourself – read, listen to music, and browse the internet. Always expand your knowledge in your domain. Information is everywhere, stay caught up.[6]

COPYWRITING & COMMUNICATIONS

361. The font you choose fundamentally determines the words you write and the perspective in which you write the words.[36]

362. The value attached to copywriting is less than what it should be.[36]

363. There's no use to have a good idea if you can't explain or sell it. The opposite also applies, an idea that cannot match the time, the culture, or the client, even if it is a good idea, isn't. It's always a question of the right idea the right time.4

364. The hardest part is getting your copy and take-away message right. You could spent a lot of time and money creating an advertising campaign trying to get your brand message across, only to have only half of your intended message get picked up by the press, and that half could even be the least important part of your campaign.[31]

365. If your communication doesn't work, it's your fault. Therefore it's in your best interest to have perfected communication to eliminate all things that are in your control.[2]

366. In copywriting you must understand the difference between translations and adaptations. It's one thing to translate a document; it's another thing to adapt it. When you're adapting a document you're actually keeping the meaning but you're changing all the language in it so that it sounds as fetching as it was when it was first written, or even better.

Why spend all your money on advertising campaigns and website creation. But then all of the sudden get really tight about another language version of your documents, reluctant to pay somebody a little bit extra to translate and write it properly. Why spend all that money on a good website if you're not going to put good material on it? So in effect you have these foreign companies competing against American and British competitors spending a fortune creating impeccably designed brochures written in shoddy English being sent all around the world to potential clients.[36]

367. Sometimes you have good copy what sells a lot and it's impossible to explain why. Sometimes all the tests and product testing looks positive but the ad ultimately fails. That's the magical part of advertising: Luck and chance. The right message at the right moment.[33]

368. If you're launching a unique product or service then you may have your own special keywords, but if your product or service has the same keywords as millions of other websites; it's more complicated and your site will be drowned.[35]

369. Don't neglect form over content. Even if you have strong ideas and very good solutions, one of the issues you need to deal with is the way you're presenting your ideas. It's one thing to have a good idea, but you also need to be good at explaining and presenting it.[7]

370. Most of the time, if you handle yourself transparently, apologize for your mistakes, and offer to make any wrongs right, people can't be angry with you afterwards.[24]

371. Marketing and communication are crucial components to the success of a brand. Look at successful companies today, their branding, marketing and communication strategies are impeccable, consistent, and easy to grasp in 30 seconds or less.

Be extremely consistent. Think of every communication you send as branding, no matter what you do. Portray the same consistent image and communication with the same message.[22]

372. If your message isn't clear in your own organization, it can't be clear for your customers. Train everybody who picks up the phone, sends an email, and interfaces with the public so that they fully understand the branding guidelines and standards for your image and product(s), and that these guidelines cannot be changed.[22]

373. Never take for granted the importance of proper grammar and spelling. It's extremely important to write without spelling and grammar mistakes.[25]

374. There are words that jump out at you and others that don't. There are sexy and beautiful words, and you can spend a long time hesitating over one word. If you're not happy or if you get stuck on a word, skip over it and keep going and then come back to it when you have the idea when you've a better grasp of the rest of the text.[36]

375. Consider an article title you could reasonably encounter online nowadays: "*10 Life-Changing Cat Videos. Number 6 is insane!*" The author's copywriting objective of creating the maximum amount of interest in the shortest amount of time possible, and obviously the author added "Life-Changing" solely as a hook to get more clicks. Readers will most likely click the article out of sheer curiosity while understanding that cat videos won't be life changing.

This parasitical and manipulative title may be successful in the short-term, but if the rest of the article is no good, then the short-term success could be to the detriment of the author's, and by extension the website's, long-term credibility.[36]

376. Increase investor awareness by bringing out the right message at the right time. When companies publish results, analysts and investors might begin by turning to the company's website and press page for information.[28]

377. Consistent, friendly and purposeful communication across multiple channels is crucial.[43]

378. Marketing is the window for the world into your company. People judge individuals they meet in the first 30 seconds of meeting them for the first time, and brands are the same. If your messaging is wrong or the way you present your image is inadequate, then you've failed before you've even started. Learn your business and learn your pitch.[22]

379. Get out there and promote yourself. People aren't going to magically find you and give you money and promote you for free. You have to promote yourself – hand out flyers, advertise on Facebook, etc. Create a community and promote sales and giveaways. A website is useless when nobody knows you exist.[60]

380. There's a plethora of information out there, so the problem becomes distinguishing yourself from all the information and attracting attention. You do that by bringing out the right message at the right time, and to do this you have to be spot on.[28]

381. Information isn't distributed evenly- it's not a perfect liquid market.[28]

PUBLIC RELATIONS

382. Your marketing and public relations (PR) should be done in coordination with any advertising campaign that you run, but advertising and public relations often work side-by-side as part of a greater overall communications strategy.[29]

383. Investors aren't really interested in what a company said about its Q1 results which came out a few months ago; investors are more interested in what the company said about their Q2 results which came out three weeks ago. And three weeks from now no one will really care about that either.[28]

384. PR, like advertising, shouldn't be a one and done campaign, something that you turn on and off, and then hope it worked.[29]

385. A goal of 1,000,000 new visitors isn't going to be accomplished with a single PR release. But if your goal as an up-and-coming blog or newly started business is to get your name out there, then landing a guest blog post on a highly-ranked and highly-trafficked website definitely accomplishes introducing you to potential readers and consumers as well as jump-starts your brand's reputation.[29]

386. There are PR people out there who are in it for the money and will write whatever you want them to write whether it's true or not, but building your brand reputation based on lies isn't a good long-term strategy.[29]

387. The worst thing you can do as a brand that sells a product or service is to not think about PR at all. You've spent so much time making your product or service and website good, why wouldn't you think about how you're going to promote it?[29]

388. Good PR agencies will have good references, good contacts within their industry, and good samples of their work available upon request. Anyone can write a press release, but can they turn that press release into interviews and articles?[29]

389. If you ask around about a PR agency and no one has heard of them, that's not a good sign. A PR agency should be familiar to people.[29]

390. One time press release options will produce a lot of one-time short-term traffic, but then maximizing your conversion rate ultimately depends on:

a. How interesting your website is
b. How interesting you are
c. How good your content or product/service is
d. How relevant your content is to the visitor

e. How accessible your social media and subscribe buttons are.[29]

391. Online publications are very, very demanding and require writers to put out fresh content constantly. So people in that industry are much more likely to *'run with it.'* Therefore there is no such thing as *'off the record.'* If you say something, it's out there.[29]

392. For maximum effectiveness, your PR should work hand-in-hand with the your marketing calendar, so that press releases are published exactly as marketing is being done.[25]

393. When a journalist mentions you, it's acceptable to try to start a relationship with the journalist by contacting them saying *"Thank you for quoting or mentioning me, it really helped my traffic. Maybe we can have coffee sometime."*[25]

394. When journalists write special articles on your brand's particular industry, when you launch a new product, or just to make sure you're quoted very often in the newspapers, work to make sure the journalists talk positively about you.[25]

395. In times of crisis, ensure the situation has been well explained to journalists and that no misleading, unverified information is published.[25]

396. For positive stories you must negotiate and pitch the story to the journalist and explain why it's interesting. This involves working hand-in-hand with journalists and pitching in such a way that they want to write about you. There's a lot of psychology behind it: understanding how someone works and what their and their readers are interested in.[25]

397. You cannot buy journalists. However PR agencies can provide journalists with access to clients they normally would not have and provide them with exclusives. There is win-win force ratio - the journalists and PR agencies try to work with each other.[25]

398. You may find yourself in a bad situation, but what the general public may not know the exact reasons as to why. So journalists listen to PR agencies because there is a sort of compensation. Not with all journalists, of course. There are some who work on investigation alone.[25]

399. In the PR industry people can think that they can write articles for journalists, or that companies think it's easy for a PR agency to get the journalists to write what the client wants them to write about. Remember that you cannot buy journalists. It's all about preparation, explanation, and relationship. Understand the environment, context, and pressures around the journalists.[25]

400. PR is not just about advertising. The difference between advertising and PR is that PR gives more credit for you to be quoted in an article because it's not viewed as advertising.[25]

401. Press releases are only a very small part of PR. PR is finding the right way to enter each key publication. Sometimes it's a press release, sometimes it's a meeting, sometimes it's a trip, and

sometimes it's allowing the journalists to meet people. It can be a lot of things.[25]

402. To create relationships with the key journalists, press releases are but one technique. Instead of sending the press release and then calling the journalists, organize a meeting with journalists letting them know that a press release will be released next week, and that they have a chance now to meet with several key client figures to ask questions beforehand. Even offering exclusives is but a small part of PR. When it's big public information and everyone needs to have the information at same time that you cannot do exclusives.[25]

403. Release bad news quickly and good news slowly.[25]

404. PR should be more about advice than about a service. That is how you bring more added value to what you do at the end of the day.[25]

405. Don't develop an obsession with being mentioned in a specific column on a specific page of a specific newspaper. It's a lot about competitive monitoring: watching what's happening in your industry and with your demographic around the world. It's a question of being alert to your environment.[25]

406. Sometimes brands want to please journalists so much that they're ready to talk bad about their competition and use 'off the record' when they shouldn't. The idea of 'off the record' isn't the same for the client as it is for the journalist. For a journalist, 'off the record' means they can use the information you gave them, but they can't quote you directly as the source. For the client, *'off the record'* means the journalist won't use the information at all, which is completely useless when you think about it. Why say something to the journalist if you don't want him to use it? You either don't say anything or you say it. It's kind of a tricky game. You can usually identify 'off the record' statements in articles because they're sourced by *"according to a source familiar with the subject."*

'Off the record' can also be one way of negotiating with a journalist. *"Look, my clients worked on a particular transaction you're writing an article about. If you mention my client in the article, I'll give you accurate information about the deal."*

Going 'off the record' is all on trust. Sometimes you say 'off the record' stuff, but if two or more people confirm it, then the journalist might use it on the record.

If 'off the record' information finds its way on the record, it might be a month or two of not talking with the journalist afterwards, but at the end of the day, depending on the status and the power of the publication the journalist works for, you need the journalist.[25]

407. You can't do PR and not read the newspapers and magazines. You have to understand who writes about what.[25]

408. A lot of people aren't very good at promoting and advertising themselves. If you search for your name on the internet and your personal profile and website isn't the first to show up – or isn't even on the first page – then you really need to work to fix that immediately.[51]

409. Success is mostly through contributors outside of your social network. You're able to reach a lot of folks all over the world through interviews and blog features.[43]

COMPETITIVE ADVANTAGE

410. Stronger and more established competitors will always be able to offer similar products and services as you do, but at a cheaper price. So focus instead on building and strengthening your brand image. Brand image isn't easily replicated.[35]

411. Read competitor's websites and what other copywriters and authors have written about your particular topic. Read a lot; that's where you get a lot of your language and inspiration.[36]

412. The less money you have, the more creative you have to be with the limited resources you have. This can be a good thing if you're creative. It means that nobody else is doing what you're doing.[32]

413. Read your competitor's websites to get an idea of the terminology and language they're using, and then adapt it to your brand.[36]

414. Identify the top websites in your sector and deconstruct each website's logic. Prosperous brands organize their websites and social media platforms on the advice and research of very expensive media agency studies, advice, and data. Reverse engineer their behavior and use it to your advantage. There's nothing wrong with incorporating and adapting what the top websites are doing.[40]

415. Your competitors probably spend a lot of money on advertising, and it's possible that your 'disruptive' packaging may catch the consumer's eye and they may even choose your product out of sheer curiosity. You may even lure them into purchasing your product instead. But product design cannot replace advertising, and the chance that consumers will actually choose your product over their usual product purchase is rare. This is partly due to the fact that most consumers simply purchase what they're familiar with; the brands and products they have 'always bought before'- consumers really need an incentive to change their habits and try something new.[46]

416. Established, dominant brands enjoy a huge advantage in the marketplace. Competing head to head on the same turf as your competitor rarely works.[44]

417. A company who's CEO is well known (in good way) and conveys the right message - embodying their company strategy and way of operating - brings added credibility to the company compared to its peers.[28]

418. If you're in an industry where customer expectation is low, then it doesn't take much effort to stand out from your competition.[44]

419. There is a great opportunity for brands willing to take risks because you'll stand out in your industry and stay in the consumer's mind longer, which ultimately leads to a larger return on investment for your risk.[49]

420. Inform yourself and understand the business and the industry you're competing in.[60]

421. There are emerging opportunities waiting to be exploited every day; all you have to do is find and use them to catapult your brand to success. It's all about identifying emerging opportunities and then exploiting them to grow your business and grow your community before every else figures it out and saturates the market and before policy changes go into effect.[57]

422. Align your brand with the objectives of your consumers in your industry to set yourself apart from your competitors and help make your client's lives better in some way. If you're trying to establish a business, find out if there is a market for what you've got, or be able to successfully create the need.[2]

HOW CAN I CREATE MY OWN INSPIRING CREATIVE BRIEF?

Download our free 65 question strategic planning & creative brief template at www.humanbehavior.solutions

423. Everything comes from your creative brief. The quality of your campaign is directly reflected in the quality of your brief. Vague and imprecise briefs cost brands and agencies precious time and money in the idea brainstorming phase, and the final advertisement will probably not be something that everyone involved is happy with.[47]

424. An important element of a good creative brief is having a clear vision.[49]

425. Preparing a high-quality, comprehensive, and targeted branding strategy is extremely important because it leads to a high-quality branding and advertising campaign.[34]

426. Come up with a kickass creative brief and a good idea (which is the most difficult bit). That is the secret to powerful campaigns, regardless of how much money you have.[47]

427. The best creative briefs are when your creative team leaves the brief meeting with ideas already in their head. If your brief is boring, or leaves your creative team with more questions than answers, or worst, demotivated, then your creative brief was a failure. Include just enough information to spark creativity- you should be able to accomplish this in one page.[42]

428. Even before the client can ask an agency to do anything, everything starts with the creative brief. Agencies need to know:

    a. What product(s) you want to advertise and why
    b. The context: who is your target demographic and who are your competitors
    c. Any limitations (budget, time, legal obligations, etc.)
    d. Your unique selling point (USP) and reason to believe (RTB)[39]

429. Generally, you come at the creative brief from three directions:

    a. What does your brand want?
    b. What do you think the consumer wants?
    c. What do you as the art director believe is the best approach?

Then, you will choose the approach you like best. Often times it's a mash up of the three.[45]

430. When creating a brief, it's crucial to precisely identify the brands needs because clients won't always tell you directly during the initial meeting. You have to be able to read between the lines.[49]

431. Your goal is almost always the same:

    a. How to show my product/service is the most technologically-advanced?
    b. How to show my product/service is the best quality?
    c. How to show my product/service has the best return-on-investment?
    d. Etc.

A brand's goal is almost always the same, that's why your question needs to be so sharp. Advertising shows the answer to the same question, but the answer is different for each brand. However it is possible to have a marvelous question but there isn't a creative answer for it - it is possible that the question is so sharp that you'll have a small answer.[17]

432. The most important difference between good advertising and bad advertising is the quality of your creative brief. A good brief won't always guarantee a good advertising campaign, but a bad strategy will almost always guarantee a bad advertising campaign. So invest the most of your time and money on creating the best possible brief you can before you invest a single penny on the advertising implementation.[48]

433. If your creative brief can apply to any of your competitors, or to any other company, then your strategy isn't good enough – it must be very specific to your brand/product/service.[48]

434. Before you do anything, your main question must be *"What is my story? What am I trying to accomplish?"*[32]

435. The shorter your creative brief, the better. If it's too long, then your work isn't good enough. One to two pages maximum. You have to focus on the problem you need to solve.[33]

436. Costs accrue on projects when you change things at the last minute after production is underway.[27]

437. Some brands approach consumers from an emotional POV *("We want to be known as a luxury*

brand") and some from a business POV *("We have to sell X number of sweaters.")*. During your creative briefing agencies want to find out what your brand really wants, so agencies ask *'why,' 'how,'* and *'what are you really trying to do?'*[26]

438. While people always make mistakes, planning can save a lot of headaches and maximize your budget.[27]

439. A good idea doesn't necessarily require a budget.[27]

440. Focus on the planning stages - getting your target and your message correct before moving forward is vital.[27]

441. Brands began because somebody loved to do something, because of humor or love or irony. As your brand grows you should tell your story to people who may not be familiar with your brand's origins. Determine your brand's original story's emotions and infuse that emotional aspect to your advertising campaign, no matter how practical or analytical the objective.[26]

442. Aim for creating an emotional attachment in your writing.[36]

443. Television commercials may be 30 seconds long, but you have less than 5 seconds to capture the consumer's attention or the remaining 25 seconds of the commercial will be ignored.[48]

444. Print advertising is different than television advertising because you have to capture and surprise at the same time, and it has to be immediate.[48]

445. Advertising, honestly, doesn't change much. The same techniques used in advertising of yesteryear are pretty much the same techniques used today. What's different is the inspiration, things at our disposal and the way we present the advertising to consumers.[48]

446. As a rule of thumb, don't put too much information in your creative brief because too much information and facts can actually hamper inspiration and creativity. For creatives, keep your brief to one to two pages max.[42]

447. Create a brief that best interprets your needs in an inspiring way so that you can meet those needs in the most creative way possible.[27]

448. Asking the right kinds of questions is key. Don't be afraid to be inquisitive, listen carefully to what your client wants to fully understand their reasoning behind it. Another important factor is understanding the target audience. The absolute worst thing you can do is assume you have it all figured out and then bring offer a solution people didn't ask for - not only will you have wasted their time and money, but also yours. You must thoroughly make sure you and your client are on the same page from the outset so that what you produce is what they want.[27]

449. Your creative brief outlines your problem: *"We want to sell more cars,"* or *"Our brand reputation is bad."* After that nothing else matters. There are no bad briefs.[51]

450. For your initial creative brief, don't go into too much detail. State what your end goal is for the campaign and then leave plenty of room for creative imagination.[60]

451. Start by doing a search and seeing what people have said/are saying about your brand, your competitors, and your industry.[50]

452. There's a lot of information available online, so you don't want to waste time asking people questions you could easily find online.[42]

453. Before you prepare your creative brief, do a search on your brand just to get a general overview of who you are and where you're coming from as well as the perspective of your search results from your consumer's perspective. Look at your brand's website, history, search results, your competitors, etc. Doing this before you've even created your official brief helps for three important reasons:

   a. It allows you to view your brand objectively as a casual consumer and not as a creative working for your brand.
   b. After you've created your brief, you can compare your previous findings with your brand's objectives.
   c. With the general search out of the way, you can narrow your search and focus on idea generation.[58]

454. Corporate strategy is more about your brand philosophy and image of your group and the perception you want your overall brand to have today, tomorrow, in five years... Corporate strategy would talk about innovation or social responsibility; issues higher than your business.[34]

455. International strategy tends to be about communicating on a particular subject to develop your brand as an expert in that subject. Being in the right place in the right time in an international context.[34]

456. Your brand may incorporate B2C, B2B, corporate and international strategies, and the branding strategy you focus on determines which kind of media you advertise and communicate on. For example, journalists for business magazines will be more interested in corporate and B2B news. While bloggers and social websites would be more interested in the B2C advertisements.[34]

457. There are a thousand things beyond your control that can cause an advertising campaign to not meet its objectives: bad timing, unanticipated events, etc. But much of the time if your advertising or branding campaign doesn't meet your objective, the blame falls on an incomplete branding strategy research.[34]

458. Strategic planning involves handling the research aspect of your idea creation and offer proposals so the creative team(s) know which directions are available to them. But ultimately you should go with your gut feeling. If your gut feeling differs from the research, or if your creative team finds a better way to solve the branding strategy, then that's great. From the advertising agency's perspective, the objective is to solve the client's problem.[34]

459. Most agencies hire strategic planners whose sole responsibility is to create the strongest creative brief possible and ensure that the idea in the brief isn't lost through the various stages of the creative process.[47]

460. A hybrid car company's main concern is to convince consumers to *"at least give it a try."* It will not help the creative team to create an advertising campaign aimed at increasing sales, even if increasing sales is your final goal. Instead, the more specific objective for the campaign should be to get the consumer to *"Just try it."* This is a minor detail, but that clarification in the foundation of your creative brief changes the entire course of your advertising campaign. But you can't just simply ask consumers to try it. Instead, say something that entices the consumer to try it. Your end result: more sales due to a high conversion rate, however the underlying message is significantly different.[42]

461. More and more brands want to sell an experience, not just simply products. You can find products anywhere; now brands want to sell experience and emotion. That is their main goal.[49]

462. There is the conventional way of thinking and there is disruption. If you're doing the same ads as other brands, it doesn't work. You need to be different.[17]

463. Advertisers play with codes. You are trend searchers, and you must understand before everyone else which trends are going to exist tomorrow and use them to make sure that once a trend is born your brand can use them to communicate with your consumers.[39]

STRATEGIC PLANNING

464. An important element of a good brief is your brand's story. Every brand has its own story. By telling your brand's story you create advertising that separates your brand from your competition.[49]

465. Ultimately your question is *"How well do I understand the perspective of my target demographic?"* If you can get that from browsing the internet, that's great.[55]

466. What are you building? What category are you in? Being clear about your category helps you know who you're serving, focuses on meeting real needs, and helps shape how you describe what you're actually offering. Language matters.[55]

467. Why do you exist? What is your purpose? If design is the rendering of intent, then the "Why" is the intent of your organization that needs to be present in every interaction. A successful "Why" statement articulates the intent of your organization - how are you going to transform your category? The consumer?[55]

468. Look at all of the packaging you've ever used as well as your competitors. What colors, symbols, and shapes are used? Why? What do they mean? This allows you to get an overview of how your industry has defined itself, and what packaging conventions you could disrupt or work on to differentiate your brand from your competitors.[46]

469. Begin with research and analytics. Organizations such as TNS Sofres and Ipsos, to name a few, conduct studies and compile information into reports that are available - some for free and some through a membership account.[42]

470. When you're a small business, branding and storytelling are more important than advertising because that is the most powerful way to differentiate yourself from your competition.[49]

471. The more time you have to work on your branding strategy, generally the better it will turn out.[48]

472. If you can't build your advertising campaign around your brand's personality, then build your advertising campaign around emotion.[48]

473. Competent and experienced account managers can create a good brief in as little as an hour.[49]

474. When strategic planners meet with clients, they pay attention to how you answers their questions:

    a.   They pay very close attention to the nouns, verbs, adverbs, and adjectives you use to describe your product, your consumers, etc.

    b.   Do you speak of coffee shops, single mothers? etc.?

    c.   What makes you lose sleep at night?

    d.   What do you believe is important to your consumers?

    e.   How do people react and interact with your product?

    f.   How far are you willing to go to meet your objectives? Are you risk-adverse?

    g.   Can the strategic planner have a prototype or example of your product/service?

    h.   What emotional experience do you want your consumer to have after having used your product/service?

    i.   If consumers don't buy your product/service, what would they buy instead of it?

    j.   What is your unique selling proposition?

    k.   What is the emotional message of your product/service?

    l.   Where will consumers be able to purchase/obtain your product/service?

    m.   What type of font, typography, and logo do you use?

    n.   How is your product/service constructed?

    o.   How does your product/service compare to your competitor's?

p.   How does your current product/service fit into the long run of your brand?

q.   Can your product/service be broken down into smaller, more digestible, packages?

r.   Can your product/service be bundled together into bigger, more expensive packages?

s.   What images could be used to illustrate your brand or product/service?

t.   What is your product design and packaging?

u.   What are your actionable business objectives?

v.   How many products would you like to sell?

w.   How is your product distributed?

x.   How much does your product cost?

y.   How is your product/service made available to your consumers?

z.   What up-sells, down-sells and different purchasing options can/do you offer consumers?[42]

475. Create your brief based on your brand's:

a.   Past branding strategy

b.   Current goals and objectives

c.   How your current brand image fits into your future branding strategy.[34]

476. Some major sections you should include in your creative brief are:

a.   **The Context.** Brands may seek out new branding strategies for many reasons:

- An issue with your product or product line
- A bad reputation among users or in the press
- Prices
- Etc.

Therefore, the first questions you should ask yourself are:

- *"What is your brand's main problem/ objective? What is the problem you want to solve?"*
- *"What is it about your brand that keeps you up at night?"*

b. **The Objective.** You should define a clear, concrete, and actionable objective. *"Changing the mind of the consumer"* is too generic and isn't active enough. You need to know what precisely you want your consumer (potential or already loyal consumer if you're preparing a customer relationship management campaign) to do:

  - To make a change in their life?
  - To purchase your product more often?
  - To step into a store and to take your product into their hands?
  - To give you their email address and contact information?
  - To taste your product for the first time?
  - To share your product with their friends?

c. **The Strategic Message.** Building upon your context, define your brand's strategic message. What does your brand want to say? A generic and uncreative tagline for toothpastes would be *"A perfect smile."* But this tagline applies to 100% of the toothpastes on the market - there is no superior value from this claim. So determine exactly what your brand's competitive advantage is and how this advantage makes sense to your consumer.

d. **The target audience.** Who exactly are you going after? What is your brand's current general perception of the target demographic and how can you discover and take advantage of opportunities with that target audience? Consider the cultural barriers preventing the consumer from hearing your message.

Gathering this research allows you to build a stronger creative brief to ensure that your creative team will reach your target audience precisely when they are most receptive to receiving your brand's message. Once you've defined the consumer's path, it might be a good idea to include any existing creative campaigns that use the same touch points your research uncovered to make your creative brief more inspiring.

e. **The message tonality**. Is your branding message intended to be funny, professional, mature, serious...? That's an important answer you have to have.

f. **Client limitations and constraints.** Clients may impose limitations such as creative limitations, legal issues, time constraints, or to be shot or filmed in a desert...

g. **Form.** Is your advertising campaign a television commercial, radio spot, digital, a magazine spread or print ad, a mobile application, etc.

h. **A hands on experience.** Construct a typical consumer's journey - "A day in the life of" - from the moment your product/service falls into the conscious awareness of your potential consumer to when the consumer actually tries your product out to when the consumer becomes a brand ambassador of your product. What are the steps involved? Walk yourself step-by-step through the consumer journey to better understand how consumers think, any sticking points that prevent the consumer from engaging with your brand or product more deeply, and how your branding strategy and advertising campaigns could address those sticking points.[42]

477. Dig into surveys and discussion boards to get the sense of conversations and see what people think about your brand and industry.[13]

478. There are two kinds of trends:

    a. **Classic trends:** Observing everyday people in the street, talking with the younger generations and surfing YouTube are perfect for identifying classic trends.

    b. **Prospective trends:** YouTube isn't the right process because once you go to YouTube it's already too late; you have to look elsewhere. Most of the time prospective trends are in technology and, I know it sounds kind of crazy, but prospective can also be found in science fiction books.[39]

YOUR TARGET AUDIENCE

    a. What is your target audience?
    b. How old are they?
    c. How much do they earn?
    d. What are their defining habits?
    e. Where do your consumers spend most of their time?
    f. What is their mindset or lifestyle?
    g. Can your target audience(s) be broken down into even smaller niche audiences?
    h. What about your product/service would make a consumer talk about it to their social network?

i. How does the consumer interact with your product?
j. Where must they go to obtain it?
k. What is the consumer's opinion about your brand and category?
l. What do you know about your target demographic?
m. Are you B2B or B2C?
n. If you don't know much about your target demographic, conduct consumer studies – either by an agency, by yourself, or by a third party.
o. What are your deadlines?
p. What is your budget?
q. What are your constraints and guidelines?
r. What are your communication and marketing objectives?[52]

479. Research your competitors and complimentary brands to see how they're branding and communicating their image and product.[34]

480. Your main goal is a satisfied customer.[55]

481. Thoroughly identify your different visitor's profiles. Group your visitors into as many relevant segments as you can. Create profiles for each visitor segment and keep them on the wall next to your computer. This allows you to stay focused as you deepen your website content and to identify potential collaborations - vertical or horizontal - you could make.[40]

482. Dive into your consumer's mindset and understand how they feel and interact with your brand.[42]

483. At some point in your advertisement you have to surprise the consumer, but you have to surprise them before they get bored, otherwise they'll ignore you before they have been surprised.[48]

484. Funny messages tend to be more successful than non-funny messages.[48]

485. With print ads your idea must be very concise; consumers must understand your advert in 3-5 seconds. With commercials, short-films, and videos the idea has to be in story form.[51]

486. Consumers do not have answers; they have experiences. Yet most consumer research approaches people as if they were a source of reliable answers to our questions, and that consumers keep those answers in our heads. This is a disastrous misunderstanding.[55]

487. Conduct men and women's groups separately, partly because all categories are gendered, and partly because men and women communicate differently when they're in the company of the other.[55]

488. Do not have anyone introduce themselves at the beginning of consumer research groups. This helps to avoid the creation of a social hierarchy that arrives as soon as you know what neighborhood someone lives in, or job they have.[55]

489. The mind thinks in images first, so do a lot of free association and projective questions to get at the imagery and emotions and work backwards. All the exercises should be written down to give people the opportunity to free associate within themselves and to protect against social influence.[55]

490. Brand listening needs both conversation and observation. In conversation, all listening should be oriented towards the embodied experience with your brand through indirect questioning, deep metaphor exploration, and projective exercises to get at motivations, mindsets, values and imagery. Observation should be about shared experiences to understand the context.[55]

491. Who are you serving and who is your ideal prospect? How do you define the activities people are already doing that make them most likely to see the benefits you are offering? Actual experience in a category of behavior is a better predictor of future behavior than any demographic information.[55]

492. Sometimes what people say they want and what they actually want are two different things. There may be incredible insight hidden in-between the lines on your creative brief, and if you don't identify it, then you may miss some real opportunities.[47]

493. It is not the job of your customer or prospect to answer your marketing questions.[55]

494. Who you talk to matters. Don't talk to friends and family. Recruit your interviews according to the behaviors of the category that matters for your business.[55]

495. Try to stay away from doing group consumer studies. Do one-on-one interviews instead if you can. If you do not know how to manage a group, you will be overwhelmed.[55]

496. Listen widely. Give people space and time to describe their own experiences and stories they have had.[55]

497. Be patient. Don't interrupt. This will be harder than you think.[55]

498. Give your full attention. Eye contact and body language matter immensely.[55]

499. Either give your consumers a full experience or don't. You can't take back a bad or incomplete experience. Have either a functioning prototype or a minimum viable story.[55]

500. Stay away from the future. Asking people what they might do in the future is unreliable.[55]

501. (when asking questions) Stay away from money. Paying money hurts. Avoid causing pain.[55]

502. Ask open-ended and indirect questions. Practice starting every question with "What" or "How."

   a. "What's interesting about the product?"
   b. "How does this feel different?"
   c. "What is this like?"
   d. "What does this remind you of?"
   e. "How would you describe that?"[55]

503. Avoid asking 'Why' questions. This puts people on the defensive and assumes there's a rational explanation.[55]

504. Do not introduce your own language. What you call something and what they call something could be totally different. It is this difference that creates insights.[55]

505. Ask follow up questions. The first response is never a complete response.[55]

506. Ask about their language. Listen for emotional or descriptive words. Follow up by simply saying their words back to them.[55]

507. If you find someone explaining something instead of describing something, it's probably not the whole truth. Focus on getting descriptions.[55]

508. Get really comfortable at being in the presence of other people and asking them to describe their experiences.[55]

509. You listen to consumers when you need inspiration or if you need to refine. [55]

510. At the early stages of any development, your goal is to explore the category through the eyes of the consumer in order to inspire ways of thinking about opportunities.[55]

511. For your advertising campaign to be successful, you must be able to think like the consumer in front of the TV (or wherever it is your advertising appears). The problem is that you the brand owner may have too much stuff in your head to be able think clearly and dispassionately - it's next to impossible to think like the consumer in front of the TV with too much in your head.[17]

512. For each text copy you write, understand who your audience is and then challenge them. If your content is too easy, consumers won't think about it afterwards. If it's too difficult, they'll give up on it.[36]

513. Brands without an in-depth branding strategy require a lot of work to familiarize themselves with their industry, branding environment, and their consumer and require constant monitoring of their environment to stay up-to-date with their industry.[34]

514. Don't automatically take what people say at face value. People change their minds a lot. Also situations and research changes people's perspectives all the time. Listen to what people say, but trust yourself to do a good job and go with your gut, then find a balance.[47]

515. Consumers in the B2C industry tend to be less loyal than consumers in the B2B industry. B2B tend to be more interested in and responsive to facts and figures, return-on-investment, and are more rational than B2C. B2C tends to be more responsive to humor, emotion, and seduction; B2C companies focus on finding new ways to make their existing consumers more loyal.[34]

516. Create what your audience is asking for.[56]

BRAINSTORMING FROM THE CREATIVE BRIEF

517. All work begins with a spark. Whether you want to burn down an entire city or the whole world - it all begins with a spark.[17]

518. With each question you can have +1,000 answers.[17]

519. Every advertising campaign begins with a question - the problem that the advertising campaign has to solve. Having the right question saves a lot of time in the creative process. Once you have the right question, coming up with the right answer is very simple, it's communication.[17]

520. *What did you discover this week?* If you don't have an answer to this question, get out of your office and don't come back until you've discovered something.[39]

521. Rewrite your creative brief to make sure you fully understand what you want before you begin working on the answer. This allows you to note the most important words in the brief as a reference point.[46]

522. When you work on the computer you need to save your progress as you go. Therefore you need a sort of numbering system to keep track of your progress and your most recent work. Every big change you make to your advertising campaign in the production process should be saved under a new name instead of keeping the same document and saving on top of it, but it's rare you will go back to previous ideas because changes are made for a reason and ideas develop and get better with each step.[51]

523. Every creative has his or her own unique "filing cabinet" of ideas.[51]

524. A remarkable idea is the most important. If you're creative and invest your time you can come up with a remarkable idea for free, then you can invest all of your money paying to place your idea in front of consumers. But coming up with remarkable ideas isn't easy.[58]

525. With advertising, you can't do a good job without curiosity. Creatives respond to the same exact creative brief with completely different solutions. With time you can learn to be creative, but what differentiates bad from average from good from very good creatives is curiosity and feeling.[51]

526. When looking for an idea, you can stop once you've reached an average idea, but better creatives don't stop there, they keep looking until they've discovered something truly unique.[51]

527. You could spend all day at your office racking your brain to come up with an advertising campaign without success, only to be at home watching a movie trying to fall asleep when all of the sudden the answer to your creative brief pops into your head.[48]

528. Make it a habit of keeping your thoughts organized so that you can return to your ideas in an organized fashion whenever you find yourself in a creative rut.[48]

529. You can't have any way of knowing whether a photo or graffiti or a particular line from a script in a movie will be useful to you in the future; you just can't predict those sorts of things. But the worst is when you remember having seen or heard something "at an event sometime last year" that would be perfect for a particular problem you have in front of you now, but you can't remember where you saw it and how to find it again. That is when you have that regretful feeling that you're missing out on a really incredible brand-changing idea because you didn't note it down then – even if it was just a flyer you kept from the event or a jot in your planner to help jog your memory about what you did on any particular day.[48]

530. The more time you have to generate ideas, the better your ideas will be.[58]

531. Once you have a general idea get your rough draft down on paper. It's wiser to design your rough draft with a pencil and paper before moving on to Photoshop, Illustrator, or InDesign. This is because drawing freehand is so much less constraining than working with software.[46]

532. You're never creative enough. *"You're feeling one part of the creative brief, but not the complete idea."* Sometimes you have to keep your idea longer because it's not ready yet.[17]

533. The creative process should be creative, but within the confines of what will most effectively touch your target consumer demographic.[42]

534. It's always risky to base your creativity off of too many examples and too much instruction because they can persuade you too much.[17]

535. Train your eye and your brain. You might see something that means nothing to a problem directly, but it opens something in your brain. The brain is a muscle. The more you give it, the more back it gives you. You have to feed it with everything! Everything is interesting. Eat less advertising than other stuff.[17]

536. If you work 8 hours on a brief, you'll have 8 hours of ideas. If there's another team working on same brief for 24 hours, they'll have improbable ideas. It's the difference between a lamb cooked for only 3 hours versus a lamb cooked for 9 hours. But you have to keep simplicity and never lose the scope of the question. If you work 24 hours you could lose the question you're trying to answer.[17]

537. Your mind is constantly brainstorming throughout the day, during the day your ideas are always working in the background and that's the amazing thing about the human mind. We know so little about it and the way it works. Make it a point to constantly feed your mind and ideas will constantly emerge so that by the time you've opened up your notebook you already know where you're going with your idea and you're able to just sit down and write.[36]

538. The right idea is integral to any successful advertising campaign, and most successful advertising ideas involve some degree of risk.[47]

539. During the initial idea generation phase, sketch out as many designs and ideas on paper as you can before moving to Photoshop or Illustrator because:

   a. Ideas can come to you from out of nowhere and in the most random moments and places, and it's easier to find a pen and paper than it is to find Photoshop.
   b. Ideas flow more easily and freely when you free-sketch than with computers because on a computer you're limited to Photoshop and Illustrator's user interface to flesh out your idea. This has certain limitations. With pen and paper you have no limitations.[58]

540. To sell to a consumer you shouldn't lie to or deceive them.[49]

541. Try to understand your creative brief from different angles. During the idea brainstorming phase go into your mind and revisit expositions, pictures, web sites, and videos you've seen that can mix with your product. Eventually, connections begin forming in your mind.[47]

542. It's all about your angle - your point of view from which copy is written, especially when your copy is intended to interest a particular audience.

Determining your angle involves:

a. Knowing your target audience so you know who you're talking to
b. Researching all relevant information about your product, your competition, and the problems surrounding your product
c. Determining how you want to position your brand
d. Boiling it all down into one short sentence and catch phrase you want people to take from your advertisement[31]

543. Less is more. Find the right idea and be able to summarize it in just a few words.[47]

544. 90% of your time should be invested in coming up with ideas, once you've settled on your idea, the remaining 10% of your job is implementing that idea: finding the photographers, models, location, etc.[45]

545. Consistently coming up with good ideas is mechanical. When you train for a marathon, it's hard at the beginning, but as you force yourself to run it becomes more natural. You do have the basics such as metaphors and similes or to change the point of view or perspective, etc.[45]

546. Develop your own methods through experience. Each creative has his or her own unique methods of generating ideas. But to get off on the right foot, you absolutely must have a good creative brief.[45]

547. Who you surround yourself with plays an integral role in the quality of the ideas you come up with.[45]

548. It's important to explore passions outside of your work. Working exclusively in an advertising environment isn't enough. You have to enrich your creativity and ability to generate ideas.[45]

549. Have side projects outside of advertising. Do anything and everything but advertising. It's crucial for the creative's brain to work on things other than advertising, otherwise you become stale and your creativity dries up.[48]

NARROWING YOUR CREATIVE IDEAS DOWN

550. Once creatives have narrowed down their ideas from your creative brief they are in back-and-forth meetings to further refine the idea until it is ready to be presented to you.[58]

551. Pinterest is a great image bank for finding specific photos relative to your project. Pinterest is better than a general Google photo search because Pinterest is social so the best photos tend to rise to the top.

Don't use the actual images you find, of course, because that would be a violation of the owner's copyright. But use what you find as inspiration to create your own twist.[60]

552. Your artistic decisions should benefit your brand, not your particular artistic preferences. You can add your own artistic signature in the little details, but keep in mind you're doing this project for your brand, not for yourself.[60]

553. Most brands that have a legacy and a quality of character are ultimately best experienced in person - it's primal in a way, and these experiences can be dialed up or down depending on the intent of the experience.[26]

554. Identify the mood you want to portray and then focus on crafting one amazing image with one phenomenal message and then work to get it out there in as many creative ways as possible.[26]

555. The creative process isn't linear; it's neither easy nor comfortable.[26]

556. The best ideas tend to be the simplest. Overly-complicated messages usually get diluted, and tend to do the opposite of what you wanted.[27]

Download our free 65 question strategic planning & creative brief template at www.humanbehavior.solutions

I HAVE A SMALL MARKETING BUDGET, ANY ADVICE?

557. Work with image banks such as Getty Images, Corbis, Flicker's Creative Commons License Search or Shutterstock.[60]

558. Start small. See if people are really interested enough to open their wallets and buy before you invest too much time or money into something.[59]

559. Go where your potential consumers are and link to your community.[57]

560. Regardless of whether the customer is right or not, bend over backwards and kill them with kindness, be fair and empathetic and offer to make any wrongs right. Then, if your business is based on word of mouth and referrals, for every one customer that complains, a hundred others will stand up for you.[56]

561. When guest posting on other websites, your first pitch is often a hurdle, but once you're in and people know you by reputation, it opens the door to future guest posting opportunities. Read your target website every day until you're prepared, understand their guidelines, know their target audience, and know exactly what they are looking for. Then approach them.[29]

562. Join meet up groups and do social networking. Co-publish a book. Don't JUST do things only in your niche; contribute to projects complimentary to what you offer that broaden your exposure and build your credibility and trust.[56]

563. Don't pay for advertising. Instead, see it as a challenge to keep the quality of your free content as high as possible because you want people to really like and share what they see.[54]

564. Work with freelancers - you'll get a better deal and the end product will be more or less the same.[53]

565. Email marketing, but with a limited budget Facebook ads might be better. If you're targeting teenagers or 20-35 year olds and you know your target is on Facebook, then go on Facebook because you know you'll reach them there. If you have a really large target demographic and you aren't sure if they are on Facebook, first research your consumer demographic much deeper to determine where they are. But even if you purchase a qualified database of 1,000 emails, don't expect a thousand hits to your website. Many of those emails will not be opened and many others will land in the spam file.[52]

566. Avoid spammy and pushy words like: Winner, Special offer, Free, Huge promotion, etc. When consumers see these words too often they automatically label you as spam.[52]

567. Do email marketing by creating your own database. Have a way for your visitors to give you their email address so you are 100% sure that they want to receive your email updates.[52]

568. You must support your viral campaign with paid advertising to ensure it reaches the tipping point to get spread. Purely viral content isn't really "viral" anymore because it still relies on paid advertising.[52]

569. Video truly is the king media. You could spend all your money creating a killer website and then spend hours researching and writing an incredible article, and that article will only last for one day. A good video, however, has more entertainment value, is more sought after than written content and your message will travel further and reach more people than written text will. Videos also tend to come up in conversations more often.

How often do you stop a conversation to show a person a video you saw the other day? How often do you stop a conversation to show a person a blog post you read the other day? Invest in making great videos.[52]

570. Launching a PR event and invite bloggers hoping they will write about your brand and their experience is a risk because you've no guarantee:

a. Bloggers will show up
b. Bloggers will write about your event
c. What they write about you will be positive.[52]

571. Incorporate a "submit your work" model into your website so others can have their work featured. When they are featured they will most certainly share their being featured on your website with their followers. This would be a great passive way of building a community and attracting new people.[52]

572. Your homepage is technically the biggest marketing tool brands have that you can get for free.[50]

573. Maintain consistency across your brand's website and social media sites as well as making it clear that your website is part of an overall corporate identity.[50]

574. Making it clear to your visitor that you have a solid product that you're proud of is a key goal that you want to demonstrate throughout the look and feel of your website and social networks.[50]

575. Go to a lot of social mixers and meet as many people as you can. Once you get comfortable, speak at a couple of events. Get yourself out there and start meeting people. Every single good job I've had and every single client I've had I found through other people.[50]

576. If you are at a very early stage in your business, not particularly well connected, and need to get yourself out there – throw a party and invite everyone you can.[50]

577. Focus all of your attention on creating the best creative brief you can.[49]

578. Gorilla marketing isn't expensive and young people like it because it's "illegal, but not really..." A win-win formula if your target demographic is a younger audience. But be careful! For example, it's illegal to spray paint and tag the streets with your brand name, but it's not illegal to use a high-pressure water cleaner gun and "clean the street" so that your brand name and website are visible. Make sure that whatever it is that you do is temporary and can be removed if need be. Also make sure you abide by your local laws, otherwise you could risk legal consequences.[49]

579. Depending on your product, public relations or an event around your brand or product might be more cost effective than advertising. But if it's an event people might remember the awesome night they had but not remember your brand the next day.[49]

580. Find and connect with freelancers, if they like your idea, they'll probably know or be able to find other freelancers who can help you on different aspects of your campaign. One freelancer may be good at Photoshop and not very good with video, but he'll most likely know a couple of freelancers who are good with video to send you to and who might be interested in working with you. If your idea or product is seductive to the creative, they'll be interested in working with you – even if your budget isn't very large.

Money is important for freelancers who have rent to pay, but it isn't always the number one criteria for creatives when choosing projects to work on.[48]

581. A lot of people can create their own advertising. It boils down to knowing the techniques (form), knowing your target audience (research) and presenting your idea correctly to the target audience (content).[48]

582. Make videos by yourself and upload them to Youtube.[47]

583. Creatives are always working on side projects and passions, many times for free for their friends; so befriend a creative. I often have a drink at a bar near my flat. Sometimes the bar owner gives me a free drink. So I once offered to help his business by creating a flyer to promote his bar locally.

If you can offer an interesting exchange, then creative professionals may be interested in working with you. Get out there and start building your creative social network.[47]

584. Give away a free version of your product in exchange for your visitor's email address and permission to contact them in the future.[46]

585. Instead of paying for advertising, make a cool product, put it in an eye catching package and give it away for free at the right place and let word of mouth do your advertising for you. With a unique and different packaging design, people will talk about you more. Just like that a little brand can be in competition with a global leader.[46]

586. Invest in in-store and point-of-sale ambient advertising such as hanging posters and pop-ups (displays; not internet). With pop-ups, they have to be built so that:

a. They can be conveniently folded for easy shipping to the store locations
b. They are easy to unfold and set up by store clerks who don't have a lot of time and may not even have the instruction manual to set it up; it has to practically set itself up. If the clerks and suppliers at the end of the line cannot put it together, then it will end up in the trash and all that time and advertising potential at the point of sale - arguably the most important part of the advertising process since that is where the consumer has the "moment of truth" on what they are going to purchase – is wasted. You must take all of this into consideration.[46]

587. Instead of creating a package that is simply thrown into the trash afterwards, use your budget to devise a packaging that can have a life beyond that of simply protecting your product until the consumer opens it. Preferably something that would look good on a bookshelf or somewhere in the consumer's house where friends and family can find it and ask about it.[46]

588. Find people who work in advertising agencies and tell them that you don't have much money, but that you're willing to give them 100% free reign on creativity. Most creatives, if they are attracted by your project, will jump at the opportunity to help you and work without constraints. Creatives are always looking for passions to explore outside of their work.[45]

589. An agency might be willing to get behind your campaign if they believe in it and if your ad offers them the opportunity to win an award.[45]

590. Very rarely turn down invitations to speak in front of other people, and make an effort to talk with people outside of your industry's world because the progress being made in your industry probably isn't being widely-enough shared with people.[44]

591. Most companies have *"Buy 10 of something and get one free"* loyalty program cards which you must carry around with you in your pocket and remember to have it stamped each time. Recently, one of my favorite coffee shops offered to keep my fidelity card on the wall behind their register with my name on it, and every time I came in they would stamp it for me. That's taking the idea of a loyalty program further. I'm now up on the wall and honored as a regular. That's a beautiful little psychological device - a lovely idea![44]

592. Go after your customers and make them more loyal. Never forget that customer service is relative to expectation. If you create some small unexpected element of surprise for the customer, that will make a huge difference.[44]

593. Listening to and being engaged with what people are saying about your product, brand, and service is crucial, especially when trying to raise funds.[43]

594. Staying active in your comments section and inbox is instrumental in getting funded, and continues to be a great way to stay in touch with your consumers.[43]

595. Invest your money in making and designing high-quality products that generate their own buzz. If your product/service is unbelievable, people will talk about it.[43]

596. Marketing done is important, but marketing done by real consumers is the best form of marketing. Invest your time and money in getting a video of influential people using and endorsing your product.[43]

597. Spend your time pitching to influential bloggers and journalists to get articles written about you or your products.[43]

598. Under-promise and over-deliver.[43]

599. Go directly into the street and talk to passersby within your target demographic.[42]

600. Approach people on the street and ask them to try your product and then explain their experience and opinion about your product and brand. Be more in the real life because you're talking about, and trying to market to, real people in the real life, which is more effective. Use real-life as a supplement to your strategy. Pay attention to how consumers touch and feel your product, talk about it and the verbs they use to describe it. What is their user experience?[42]

601. Instead of spending money on advertising, why not spend it on strategic planning? For example, attend an inspiring conference to fill your mind and feel the energy. This would also help you build contacts which could come in handy for you down the road.[42]

602. As a small business, you should be able to find enough information about your target demographic for free through Google.[42]

603. There's no sense in reinventing the wheel. If it suites your needs, then use what somebody else has already created.[41]

604. Brands using a multi-channel strategy and measuring the participation from each channel have greater visibility and thus greater chance of their visitors finding their way back to your website.[40]

605. If you don't have money to keep your website on the first page of your keyword searches, then at least invest in making sure your website is as SEO-friendly as possible.[40]

606. Invest your money in setting up the best analytics software you can afford or learning Google Analytics - especially the funnel options.[40]

607. When citing or quoting from other online sources, copy/paste their content as little as possible because doing so takes away from your Google ranking. Search engines consider too much copy/pasting as duplicate content and award the original post. Instead, rewrite, reword, and rephrase.[40]

608. Focus on creating permanent and positive associations between your brand with everyday objects, music sounds, and colors. Essentially, this is the ultimate objective of branding.[39]

609. Identify your niche community and identify things and ideas that your niche community all have in common, then work on permeating your brand and logo into their everyday life by attaching them to something in their everyday life and communicating around it. Being useful to people is a great door opener.[39]

610. Brands almost always use professional banner advertising, but typically as a supplement to their larger advertising campaign than as a stand-alone advertising campaign.[38]

611. This may one day change, but for now the majority of people don't use ad blocking services while surfing the web, so banner advertisements remain an effective marketing tool for brands.[38]

612. When creating a banner advertisement:

   a. Consider your banner ad as an extension of your brand, not as an advertisement for your brand
   b. Consider any investment in banner advertising as an investment in long-term branding, not just as a short-term traffic increase
   c. Most people consider pop-ups, expandable, and mouse over banner advertisements annoying, which could hurt your brand image. Don't use them unless it provides an awesome experience

d. Engage the user. Interactive banners give the person a little experience, but they can be quite expensive

e. Another way to engage your potential consumer would be to use a beautiful photo to catch their attention and evoke emotion, and draw them in. After you've engaged the user and evoked emotion, discretely include your logo so that even if people don't click on your advert, the association has been made. Next time they see your logo they'll remember it and the emotions it evoked the last time(s) they saw it[38]

613. If you're developing content which can be of interest to other demographics, consider negotiating partnerships and make "call to offers" with different brands with the objective of finding an appropriate broadcast partner. Then choose the best offer(s) and work with them. If your demographic is of interest to the content other broadcasters need to publish. Agencies will work with you, but they usually demand a guarantee of views before they give you their content and money, so you'll need to have your analytics readily available.[37]

614. On a limited budget you have to be audacious. Most brands don't take risks. This is how you can stand out, if you're daring enough.[37]

615. Communicate in the most attractive and interesting way possible in the shortest amount of time possible.[36]

616. There are many different ways of saying and portraying something, but not all of those ways will be in the best interest of your brand's overall strategy.[36]

617. Say/write things in the most attractive and catching way possible to create the maximum amount of interest in the shortest amount of time possible. That's what copywriting is all about.[36]

618. Giveaways always draw a crowd of visitors.[35]

619. Set up a knowledge-share page or forum so your readers can share their innovative projects, advice, and ideas with each other, thus creating a community.[35]

620. If you don't have the money, then don't test. Just throw it out there and see what happens. It's best to understand your target demographic as best as you can and then just trust your instinct.[33]

621. The more events you go to the more events you're invited to. You get good and bad invitations.[30]

622. Search Facebook and detect new and emerging talents to work with and use them, and push them to become more famous. Then in the next years once those emerging talents have emerged, and you caught them before, believing in them and working with them and even helping them in their rise up, they may continue working with you. You make them, they make you.[30]

623. Form partnerships and exchange your qualifications.[30]

624. Guest blogging is an excellent form of public relations and helps improve your Google PageRank. PageRank is important because it allows your website to be found organically; therefore you want to be on sites that rank highly on search engines. When looking for guest blogging opportunities, pitch to websites relevant to the topics on your own blog and that have a Google page rank of at least 5/10.[29]

625. As part of your PR campaign, find and leave meaningful comments on at least five different high Google page ranking websites in the same niche as yours per day. "Different websites" because while 15 meaningful comments on one website helps you develop a reputation on that website, those 15 comments will only count as 1 quality backlink to your website. Therefore you should also focus on finding other reputable websites to leave comments on to increase the number of backlinks to your website.[29]

626. From a PR perspective, use a blog comments plugin that gives your readers as many login options as possible. The Facebook comments plugin may be good for advertising on Facebook, but you're forcing your users to choose one platform that they might not even be part of.[29]

627. Go where your customers (current and potential) are. Set up a stand in close proximity and accessibility with customers (current and potential) so they want to interact with your brand.[61]

628. Focus on customer service relations and aftersales. Once you sign clients, focus on keeping them happy and expanding on existing services and products. Basically, do more than expected and accompany your clients and they'll stay with you for the long run.[28]

629. You don't have to use photographs. It could be art or posters - simple yet so colorful and graphic that they catch people's attention and communicate something - distinguishing you from your competitors.[26]

630. Your projects don't have to be over-the-top super expensive. They could be as simple as a typed message on a white page. Let's see if you can create one thing to be out there consistently and steadily until you can afford two pieces of communication, then three pieces...[26]

631. In cities you can do street level grass roots without over the top campaign budgets. People love to be surprised during the course of their day, and are curious enough that if they see something that sparks their interest, they'll explore it.[26]

632. Your job is 90% relationships and understanding people. Work on your communication and image of your brand. Make sure journalists and newspapers talk about your brand. Maintain separate budgets for public relations (PR) and advertising.[25]

633. Time is key. If a journalist calls you and says they're on deadline and needs certain information or someone who can comment on an issue within the next 30 minutes, you have to be able to assure or your opportunity is lost.[25]

634. You can really get journalists interested in talking about you or quoting you by contacting them directly. Journalists get interested in new initiatives. Think about what you know that could be of interest to them and then prepare your pitch. With PR you're not trying to sell a product. You're telling the journalist *"What I have to tell you is interesting because you'll be able to explain to your readers this and that"* instead of *"I want free advertising."*

Don't think about what you want the journalist to write, but what the journalist needs to write for his or her readers, and pitch that way. When you do your own job there is so much you know that others would be interested in knowing, so find the figures and statistics that you know journalists would be interested in to help them write an article. Don't try to pitch a journalist like you would pitch a consumer.[25]

When you want to be talked about, you need to know what has already been said about the subject and what still needs to be said, because it's all about thought leadership. Talk about things the journalist's readers would be interested in. You need to be new and different and bring a comparison.[25]

635. Sometimes the best way to be good is to see how others are doing, and do it differently. That's a good way to get into the press - by being different and saying something others haven't said yet.[25]

636. It's quite difficult to get major newspapers to listen to you if you don't have a PR agency, but websites and bloggers are open and more easily accessible, and it's a good way to do PR because they will appear on Google. This is becoming a new way of working with journalists where you can attract them.[25]

637. Do original market research and analysis, understand what you produce that could be of interest to journalists, then publish it and make it available for journalists to use.[25]

638. Have a press page complete with:

a. Links to all of your press releases
b. Press contact with your name, photo(s), email, and a brief bio
c. Main articles published about you. Be sure to ask for rights. You cannot scan articles or upload a pdf without asking for rights, but you can link to them.
d. A Twitter feed widget. Journalists like twitter

Once you launch a press page, it MUST be kept up-to-date.[25]

639. Propose rates and advertising packages for those who want to advertise on your website. For example, in addition to advertising space, if a potential advertiser's or investor's product and company's history has an interesting story, propose a saga and write articles about their product and company. An investor could buy some advertising space, and end up being up-sold to a 4-page article talking about the history of their company. Only propose this when there is really something interesting to write about.[24]

640. Maintain a very active social media presence and talk with your customers and followers every day. Above all, try to meet them face-to-face as often as you can.[24]

641. Do a lot of social networking: breakfast and lunch meetings, dinner cocktails with both existing clients and potential, attend industry events, etc. Spend 80% of your time out of the office networking.[22]

642. If you have small advertising budget, then save it. Unless you're selling a product that requires mass distribution to reach millions of customers, you will be better off focusing this money on your top 10 target: people you work with consistently who bring the most revenue to your firm. Building and maintaining relationships with your existing clients is the most powerful form of advertising. Focus on maintaining strong relationships so even if a competitor tries to penetrate your market share, you're protected. You'll go a much longer way spending $300 on a nice dinner with your #1 client than spending $300 on an ad in the paper or on the internet. Keep existing clients happy. It's easier to keep current clients happy than find new clients.[22]

643. Spend your money on getting client testimonials recorded on video and post them on your website. Third party acknowledgment is more powerful than all the bragging you can do.[22]

644. Don't reject sponsorship, but note that once you start cluttering your website up with ads that are not branded, it dilutes the authority of your voice.[20]

645. Speaking is where the money's at. Your products could just act as a giant business card. Conversely, you could also go and speak for free and sell your products. Either way, you should have a product with a high return on investment (ROI) for your customer, and to get the consulting gig afterwards, because that's the sustainable money.[20]

646. Submit articles that link back to your website on 30 day terms, which means the original website gets your content exclusively for 30 days. You still own the content and you can use that content on your own website after 30 days. Just pitch ideas. They're on Twitter so you can pitch ideas to them on twitter. Also you can pitch to the editor. Usually you send a

title and a summary as well as samples of your writings so they can see that you're not full of crap. If they're interested they'll get back to you; they're always looking for content. The one thing that online mediums are always looking for is content.[20]

647. Submit about 4-5 articles a month and get them distributed out on 30 day terms. Once the 30 days are up put the articles on your blog for your readership and then give your articles out to smaller blogs or affiliate partners who want your content. For the results you get it's really not a whole lot of work.[20]

648. Aim to have a few good articles rather than a lot of bad articles. Your reputation is on the line, and that's all you have in this industry. Reputation is what gets you in the door in a lot of places.[20]

649. Sometimes a simple idea such as still life or just unrecognizable people, or even a simple illustration, are easier to do and more interesting. Consider using images without models because they can be less expensive. Find a simple idea. Often the simple idea is very good.[19]

650. Buy the rights of a photographer to use just one of his/her photos already taken rather than pay a photographer to take unique photos for you.[19]

651. Get the best idea/product in your industry that can replace communication. If your product/service is unbelievable, consumers will talk about it. Marketing done is important, but marketing done by real clients is the best form of marketing.[17]

652. Come up with creative ideas for marketing, not communication. First make best product. Second

make best idea on the product. You have to be connected with your consumers by asking a lot of questions. Communication is totally natural. You ask a question and you receive good or bad answers - but it's all free![17]

653. Meet with other business owners to determine their business needs, objectives, and target goals for revenue, and then offer to make them profitable online in exchange for a percentage of profits.[16]

654. Focus on a one-to-one approach on a very targeted demographic. Make clever partnerships with other brands and exchange consumer contact details to send emails to them and bring you visibility to a specific audience.[7]

655. Don't invest so heavily in digital marketing on banners, etc. that you have nothing left to spend on brand content.

Put more money into producing quality brand content that advertises itself through word-of-mouth and less into media, or better use in media. You don't have to put a lot of money into media advertising for a viral type advertisement that's funny or useful because it advertises itself. You don't have to bring people to your campaign; people go there themselves.[5]

656. If your objective is to build a strategy to get clients, then you have to make a good quality website and make yourself known within your network.[4]

657. If you want to make yourself visible quickly, then make buzz using gorilla marketing techniques such as an action or event which will surprise people.

This way the media will write about you because of something you did.[4]

658. Be clever. It's possible to make noise with clever ideas and influential people. Seek partnerships. Focus primary attention on creating a website that draws visitors in. Then focus on pushing your site to visitors through advertising.[3]

659. Even if you're an experienced web designer, consider using a professional template to avoid the urge of spending more time modifying your website template than content creation.[16]

660. Go to advertising schools and look for talented advertising students recently graduated and partner with them. Recent grads need a portfolio to present to advertising agencies, so they'd be willing to help you in exchange for building their portfolio to get them a job.[6]

661. People always say advertising is very expensive, but you really have to have professional experts around. Until you can afford professionals, go to marketing and communication stores and read about successful case studies to learn techniques and see what has been done.[6]

662. Even if you don't have a lot of money, you really should invest in professionals to advertise for you. With the internet, everyone thinks they can do advertising or create advertising. I don't know why. It's a job that's easy to think you can do.[1]

INTERVIEW INDEX

INTERVIEW INDEX CONT.

About The Author

Joshua Smith has been an entrepreneur and freelance communications consultant since 2010. He is the owner of CadrEnglish, an executive coaching firm based in Paris, France that specializes in interpersonal communication training, and the author of How To Shape Human Behavior for startups and small businesses. He regularly lectures on communication, persuasion and interpersonal communication skills, and maintains a weekly newsletter available at:

www.humanbehavior.solutions